To Isador Zanger

SALES
PRESENTATION
TECHNIQUES
(That Really Work!)

Stephan Schiffman
America's #1 Corporate Sales Trainer

BUSINESS

Avon, Massachusetts

Published by Adams Media, an F+W Publications Company
57 Littlefield Street, Avon, MA 02322
www.adamsmedia.com

ISBN-10: 1-59869-060-4
ISBN-13: 978-1-59869-060-6

Printed in Canada

J I H G F E D C B A

Library of Congress Cataloging-in-Publication Data

Schiffman, Stephan.
Sales presentation techniques (that really work!) / Stephan Schiffman.
p. cm.
ISBN-13: 978-1-59869-060-6 (pbk.)
ISBN-10: 1-59869-060-4 (pbk.)
1. Sales presentations. 2. Selling. I. Title.
HF5438.8.P74S353 2007
658.8'101—dc22
2007010858

This publication is designed to provide accurate and authoritative information
with regard to the subject matter covered. It is sold with the understanding that
the publisher is not engaged in rendering legal, accounting, or other professional
advice. If legal advice or other expert assistance is required, the services of a
competent professional person should be sought.

—From a *Declaration of Principles* jointly adopted by a Committee of the
American Bar Association and a Committee of Publishers and Associations

Many of the designations used by manufacturers and sellers to distinguish their
products are claimed as trademarks. Where those designations appear in this
book and Adams Media was aware of a trademark claim, the designations have
been printed with initial capital letters.

*This book is available at quantity discounts for bulk purchases.
For information, please call 1-800-289-0963.*

Contents

Part Four: What Works for Presentations— And What Doesn't 103

Acknowledgments

Writing a book is a team effort. I specifically want to thank Curt Schleier for his dedication and professionalism; he was completely in tune with my thinking on the subject of sales. In addition to being a wonderful writer, he is also an excellent teacher—witness his successful business writing course delivered to corporations and governmental agencies.

I also owe thanks to Gary Krebs, Laura Daly, and Larry Shea of Adams Media, who helped shepherd this project from start to finish. My agent, Stephanie Kip Rostan at Levine Greenberg Literary Agency, was constantly encouraging.

Also key staff members at D.E.I. are due my gratitude: Ben Alpert, Scott Forman, and Alan Koval, among others, took on heavier loads so I could concentrate on this manuscript.

Of course, I'd be remiss if I didn't also acknowledge the hundreds and hundreds of former students who've stayed in touch, written in, and sent e-mails sharing their ideas and experiences with me.

Finally, last but far from least, many thanks to S.H.S., A.F.S., E.M.S., and J.R.S. for never giving up.

Introduction

It may be a little egotistical of me, but I am going to assume that if you purchased this book, you likely have heard of me. Perhaps you've seen or read one of my other books, heard me speak or taken one of my classes. This is all stuff I'm proud of. But the truth is that at my core, the thing I want written on my tombstone (when I die in about 250 years) is "He was a good salesman."

Sales is where I started, and I know sales is where I'll end. I am not a sappy guy (and I know this will sound sappy), but there is something special about the field that is difficult to describe. In many ways, it is a lonely job. You are on your own, often on the road, cold calling people you don't know, many of whom feel they are doing you a favor by seeing you for ten minutes. There are so many frustrations. But there are also incredible highs.

I've given presentations where I was in what athletes call the zone. I could see everything unfold in front of me in slow motion. It seemed the audience was mesmerized by everything I had to say, every slide I put on the screen. I knew every question before it was asked and obviously had more than enough time to formulate the right answer. It wasn't a matter of *if* they would sign a contract, only for how much.

Those sessions were the most gratifying sessions of my career because I'd created this opportunity out of nothing. I made the cold call. I had first and second meeting with prospects. I mined the company for information, gathering grist for my presentation. And then *I* put it all together.

And that in large measure is why I've written this book. I think fewer and fewer salespeople are getting to enjoy that incredible sense of accomplishment, that sense of salesperson high that I still get regularly.

I have become extremely frustrated about what I perceive is going on within the sales community. It is almost as though the "I" has gone out of the business.

I blame it all on the computer. I believe that a significant percentage of the sales-force population has come to rely on computers (and by extension PowerPoint) far too much. Specifically, salespeople use preformatted PowerPoint presentations, in part because it's easy and in part because they don't have the expertise to create presentations from scratch.

Therefore, every presentation is formatted to meet PowerPoint needs, not the needs of your customers. This has taken the creativity out of the sales process, the ability to design a program that is unique, to make it something the customer hasn't seen or heard before.

The feeling seems to be, "Well, it's in the computer, so it must be good." And sadly, that willingness to depend on outside resources rather than internal initiatives is not limited to computers. There was a very popular business how-to book published not too long ago that actually scripted sales. That is, "This is how you cold call. This is what you say at your first appointment. This is what you say on your second appointment. Here is how you present."

For a while there, salespeople were starting every conversation the same way. It made no difference to whom they were talking, what he or she was like, what product or service they were selling. Nothing mattered but following the script that was in the book.

It was what I call robotic selling and robotic presentations. That is not only counterproductive, it is to my mind counterintuitive. As far as I'm concerned, one of the beauties of sales is that you can reinvent yourself with every customer. You are one person selling to Mr. Grump and another to Mr. Easygoing. It's something different every day and on every call.

By relying on the computer to decide what you say, you are taking the human touch out of the equation. You make presentations in *person*, not via e-mail. Whether you like it or not, your personality is part of the process. It certainly won't be the deciding factor on whether or not you get an order, but it has a role. Selling is communicating, communicating your message in a way that appeals to your prospect—not in a preformatted way determined by Bill Gates.

I should point out that I'm not a Luddite. I use the computer for a number of things, and I use PowerPoint. But I use the technology to serve me. I don't serve it.

The reason I sat down to write this, its raison d'etre, is to put you back in the process, to put that individuality, that personality, that creativity, that thought process back into sales.

I want this book to be your definitive guide to making presentations. But I want it to be an aid to your process, not a substitute for it. I don't know your business. There are lessons here. You have to adopt and adapt them to your company, to your style, and to the needs of your clients.

I want you to approach this book with an open mind—the same open mind you'd like every one of your prospects to have when you call. This book was written from your perspective. I'm not some imaginary character who doesn't sell for a living. I'm someone who is real, has emotions, and goes out and prospects and sells every day.

But the advice I give you is only as good as the way you use it. If you personalize it for yourself, it will help you create better presentations and close more sales.

Stephan Schiffman
New York
August 1, 2007

Part One

Sales Presentations and the Sales Process

Chapter 1

We Hold These Truths to Be Sales Relevant

You might have heard the old chestnut that says 80 percent of a company's business comes from 20 percent of its customers. (Not surprisingly, this is sometimes called the 80/20 rule.) I don't know if that's true, but, by that logic, 80 percent of a company's business is generated by 20 percent of its sales force.

Whether those numbers are right or not—and I'm not convinced they are—really doesn't matter. The general idea, the overall concept, is certainly true. Anyone who has been in the field for more than a couple of weeks knows that the typical sales force is essentially divided into two unequal groups. The smallest group is made up of salespeople. Sadly, the largest group is made up of order-takers.

I've spent the last thirty years training salespeople—more than 500,000 by my count. And one thing I've discovered is that there is a very fine line between the haves—that is, the salespeople—and the have-nots. What's the difference between the two? One thing is desire.

The top salespeople *crave* a closing in the same way Michael Jordan yearned, no, *demanded* the ball in pressure situations and then willed it through the outstretched arms of defenders into the basket. That kind of talent is a gift from the heavens—whatever sport or pursuit you're in. It cannot be taught. You either have it or you don't. Practice can help you achieve your full potential, but that potential is ingrained somewhere in your DNA.

There is another element, however, that divides the haves from the have-nots. It can be taught and in many respects is as important as desire. Simply, it is an understanding of the sales *process*. What does that mean? It means that getting a contract signed is only the final step in a long walk. But there are a lot of steps before you reach that last one. And the path can be winding. So it's important to understand that there is a relatively easy, logical way that will get you from step one to an order.

The good news is that because you bought this book, you likely already have the desire to become a sales warrior. You understand that there's more to selling whatever it is you sell than a quick handshake. And that fills my heart with joy.

(I should point out that if you borrowed this book from a library or colleague, that you are reading it still fills my heart with joy—just not as much.)

The truth is that there is no one way to sell. How you do what you do depends upon your product, its cost, its sell cycle, and your customer's buying habits. It depends upon your position in the marketplace, and it depends on his or hers.

But all that aside, there are some universal truths. No matter the size of your company. No matter the size of your prospect's company. No matter anything.

Truth #1

The biggest obstacle a salesperson has to overcome is not the competition or price points or delivery schedules. The biggest impediment is inertia, the status quo. Your customer has been doing business in a certain way for X number of years. Unless a significant problem pops up, he's going to continue doing business the way he does. It's only natural. Your job, somehow, is to change the prospect's mindset, to prove that what you are selling is so much better, so much cheaper, so more likely to be delivered on time that it is worth her getting off her duff and initiating change.

Truth #2

Customers aren't the only ones who suffer from inertia. Salespeople do, too. They give the same canned speech, the same canned presentation to every client. It doesn't work.

For example, a few weeks ago a salesperson called on me. It was the first time we'd met. We shook hands and sat down, and he immediately launched into a completely thorough presentation . . . one with eighty-seven PowerPoint slides.

I couldn't deal with it. I knew what he wanted to sell with the second slide. But he didn't know what I wanted to buy. He never asked a single question. He thought I would be overwhelmed by his slides. I wasn't.

If I want to convince someone to use my product or service, I must make a presentation that makes sense to them—not some catch-all generic show that has little if any relevance to what the prospect does.

Truth #3

A good salesperson's goal isn't to clinch the sale—right away. Certainly getting the business is the ultimate objective. But selling is a process. The problem involves sowing seeds. You can probably harvest them before they are ready. But any farmer who does that loses the full value of his crop.

Truth #4

The biggest enemy a salesperson has is the clock. Time is limited. You have to learn how to prospect properly and to get your ratios up so that you not only get a sufficient number of appointments but appointments worth pursuing.

Truth #5

Your prospect will help you. People generally like to be helpful. If you ask the right questions, you will find the key to success. And yes, I know that sounds like a fortune-cookie aphorism—but that doesn't mean it isn't true.

The next 150 or so pages deal mainly with one aspect of the sales process: the presentation. It obviously is a key step in the process. But it does not exist in a vacuum. It is a culmination of a number of steps.

I'll be discussing each step both briefly and in detail. Over and over again. Ideally, you will make these truths your mantra. You will utter them when you wake up. You will utter them before you go to sleep. You will then clinch all your sales and thank me!

Here are some lessons to be learned from this chapter:

1. It's better to purchase my books than borrow them from someone else.

2. You cannot teach someone sales. You either are a salesperson or not. And by salesperson, I mean you're an it's-in-your-gut-and-you-have-to-clinch-that-sale-or-you'll-get-acid-reflux kind of guy or gal. However, you can learn the process. Understanding and following the process won't necessarily make you a better salesperson, but it can help you clinch more sales.

3. It's difficult to attach a weight to the different parts of the sales process. They are interconnected. So you can't really say cold calling is more or less important than presentations. If you don't make successful cold-calls, you won't be making any presentations. If your presentations stink, even the best cold-calls are moot. But certainly we can all agree that if you don't get off your duff, if you don't fight the temptation to slide through another day, if you don't pick up the phone, you might just want to go to work for the Department of Motor Vehicles.

4. Remember that your competition isn't the enemy—the status quo is. You have to show prospects that they will be more comfortable with you as a supplier than they will be sitting back and doing nothing.

5. There are just a few working hours in the day. Use them wisely.

6. It's better to purchase my books than borrow them from someone else. But you already knew that.

Chapter 2

Climb Every Mountain, Clinch Every Sale

Have you ever heard of Ed Viesturs? He is a famous mountain climber, the first American to climb the fourteen highest mountains in the world—they're all over 8,000 meters—without using oxygen bottles. How does he do it? (We'll set aside another question here, namely *why* in the world he does it.)

He plans each ascent backwards. That is, when he begins his process, he starts at the peak. Viesturs figures out when he has to leave the summit to get back to his last camp while it is still light out and by his standards safe. Once he's got that set in his mind, he then—and only then—decides when he starts his ascent.

So let's say he must leave the top at 2 P.M. to get back safely to his camp. That may mean he has to leave the camp at 1 A.M. If the weather is bad then, he'll likely cancel the climb and wait until the next day. Or the day after that. Patience is a virtue in climbing the highest mountains.

Remember: Viesturs has said many times his goal isn't to get to the *top* of the mountain; his goal is to get back *down*.

Climbing, as anyone who has tried it knows—or so they tell me, since Everest isn't on my personal to-do list—is the most vigorous and capricious of sports. You're at the whim of elements over which you don't have any control. It is physically draining. So Viesturs doesn't expend more energy by worrying how he's going to make it to the end of his journey.

When you're physically drained, it's easy to get discouraged facing a big challenge like that. So, instead of focusing on what seems insurmountable, he creates a series of incremental goals. He breaks things down to more manageable units—the rock 100 meters away, or the next step.

I mention all this because to my way of thinking, there are a number of similarities between selling and mountain climbing, and sales folks can learn valuable lessons from Viesturs's approach.

What do I mean?

Working Backwards

You can't have a battle plan until you understand what constitutes a win.

Good salespeople first try to figure out what their goals are before they meet with a client or prospect. Usually it's to close a deal of some sort—but not always. Sometimes it's just to keep an old customer from switching suppliers or get her to increase her order or use more of your product line.

In almost all cases for almost all product lines, you are going to have to make a presentation (hence this very book) before you reach your goal. But how you make the presentation and who you make it to requires research and meetings and perhaps more meetings before you actually take out that laptop.

Keeping the Proper Focus

You established your goal. Working backwards, you determined how to reach the goal and now you plan to move forward, keeping ever focused on closing the sale. Right?

Wrong.

Your focus has to be on getting to the next step. This is a *process*. Focusing on the end may put you in a position where you miss something important in the here and now.

Also, if there's a small detour on this road, thinking too far ahead can be discouraging.

For example, let's say your ultimate goal is to sign up this new client, a large manufacturer. If you can convince the prospect to use your product or service (whatever it is) you stand to reap a multimillion-dollar order. In that tiny little portion of your head where greed resides, you've already started to see little pictures of tropical drinks and romantic strolls with your spouse along Waikiki Beach.

But you've been in the business long enough not to count your chickens before someone signs on the dotted line. So you've kind of thought about what your presentation should be. You work your way backwards, to your first meeting with the prospect. You imagine the questions you will ask to gather the information you need to put together the presentation that will get you to Honolulu and perhaps a week or so on one of the outer islands.

But my question is this. What good is all that daydreaming, all your concentration on signing the deal, if you can't get past that first meeting? So while you certainly want to keep your ultimate goal in mind, what you have to concentrate on is getting to the next step in this process, whatever the next step might be. It might be a second meeting with the purchasing manager. It might be a visit to the company's plants for meetings with your product's end users. It might be a trip to corporate headquarters to sit with (and pick the brain of) the senior vice president of sales.

Whatever it is, that's what you have to focus on. In 2006, Ed Viesturs published a book about his climbing adventures titled *No Shortcuts to the Top*. Maybe I should have titled this chapter "No Shortcuts to the Sale." Because that's my main point here: You have to work thoroughly and unerringly through every step of the sales process to climb to your ultimate goal—a big sale.

Patience Is a Virtue

Like Ed Viesturs setting off to climb a mountain, you'll find that conditions aren't necessarily right every time you go out. Sometimes you have to lay back. One of my clients had an opportunity to make a sale with a very large telephone company/cell service provider. So he goes to the company headquarters and has an initial session with the appropriate people. But for reasons that are not entirely clear, he's asked to make a presentation to a larger group before he feels comfortable doing so. He hasn't had a chance to gather the information he feels he needs to make a meaningful presentation. Ideally, he would have preferred to pass.

But we don't always get a chance to work in ideal conditions. So he had no choice but to make the presentation. And just as he and logic anticipated, he didn't hit the mark. Of course, without the right information, it was pretty much impossible to hit the ball out of the park. But he hit a single. He made a good impression, just not enough that he could go on to the next step.

But he didn't do what many—if not most—salespeople do in this situation. That is, he didn't pester the prospect. Make calls and leave messages. And when that doesn't work, call at different times of the day hoping the prospect picks up the phone. And not leave messages if someone else or voice mail answers.

Don't act like you don't do it. I know you do. What my client did was bide his time. After a while, he sent an article of interest he'd seen (it was on a subject he'd discussed unrelated to business) to one of the people he met with, but other than that he did nothing. Six months later, the prospect contacted him and signed up for several hundred thousand dollars' worth of business.

What's the moral of this tale? Sometimes, like farmers, it's better to just let the land lay fallow.

So Is Flexibility

Remember the old adage about the best-laid plans of mice and men? Change is inevitable. No matter how well thought-out your plans are, someone or something will throw in a monkey wrench and screw things up. You cannot be so wedded to your plans that any change flummoxes you.

If you are not flexible, if you are locked into a speech, what do you do if someone interrupts and asks a question? Do you answer it, go back to where you were in your speech, and continue as though nothing had changed? That gives the air of being phony, of having a canned and well-rehearsed speech—and of not having taken the time to prepare something special for this client.

On the other hand, if you can roll with the punches, you demonstrate a mastery of the subject and a creativity that prospects are likely to value.

There are several lessons here:

1. You have to go with the flow. Here and elsewhere I'm going to suggest rules and approaches that will help you clinch sales. They are proven and will work 90 percent of the time. But the

only rule that is foolproof is the one that says "Rules are made to be broken." That is why it is so important to be prepared for any contingency, to be so smooth on your feet that clients confuse you with a latter-day Fred Astaire.

2. You prepare for any contingency by doing homework. Your homework is to know your prospect, your prospect's needs, and your product or service. If you've mastered that, there is nothing the prospect can throw out that will flummox you.

3. Stay single-minded. You want to make this sale, and you can only do that one step at a time. Lose sight of your goal—move to the next step—and you might just lose the sale as well.

Chapter 3

Enemies of Your Sales

There are several sales axioms that require constant repetition; to ignore them does a disservice to your employer, your family, and your wallet. Among the most important of these is that salespeople have enemies.

The first enemy is time. There are only so many hours in a day. You can only accomplish so much. To fight this enemy, you have to use your time wisely. The second enemy is the status quo. It's difficult to get people to change the way they do things—and that goes for salespeople, too. The third enemy is impatience, a desire to clinch a sale before the prospect is ready.

Battling these enemies begins when prospecting for new clients.

Most people think of sales as a numbers game. That is, the more calls you make, the greater the likelihood you get a contract signed. To a certain extent this is true. The reality is that in almost any country in the world, if you simply stand on a corner with your hand out, someone will put money in it. If you stand on the corner longer, more people will see you, so more will likely put money into your hand. But how many hours can you put in? At what point does it become the law of diminishing returns? If you are already working a full day, does it pay to stand on that corner three or four hours more when all your prospects have gone to sleep?

When it comes to begging, the numbers game alone doesn't cut it. Sales is no different. In a typical marketplace, a salesperson will get one third of the business simply by showing up. The competition gets one third. And there's that one third that is up for grabs.

I'm guessing you don't want to be the person on the corner with your hand out. So if making more cold calls won't improve your sales figures, what will? The answer is ratios—that is, the number of calls you make to the number of sales you close. Let me explain.

Every day I sell I call fifteen prospects—that is, fifteen people I've never called before. Usually I get through to seven and set up one new appointment. For every eight appointments, I close one sale. So my ratio for appointments is fifteen to one. My ratio for closing a sale is eight to one.

There are several ways I can improve my ratios. The most common approach is to play the numbers game; that is, I can cold-call more than fifteen people a day, or I can work another day of the week. Of course, the reality is that I haven't just been goofing off. There isn't any extra time in the day (or the week) for me to devote more time to prospecting.

So if just making more calls isn't a practical solution, what is? The answer is in improving other aspects of the ratio. It is not difficult. But my experience is that most salespeople don't understand ratios. Salespeople? Most sales managers don't understand ratios.

What ratios do is force you to look at what is the weakest part of your process. Remember, sales is a *process*. Do you only get through to three prospects out of every fifteen you call? Then concentrate on improving that ratio. Do you only close one sale for every fifteen prospects you visit? Then work on improving that aspect of your game.

It's easy for me to say that. But there are very simple concrete steps every salesperson can take to get through to more people, to close sales, to be more efficient. In short, to make better use of their time.

Many of these answers can be found in my book *Cold Calling Techniques (That Really Work!)*. Some of you may consider that a shameless plug. I consider it cross-selling, more information on which can be found in my book. . . . Okay, *that* was shameless.

Plugs aside, here are just a couple examples of how ratios can be improved. There are two main objectives in cold calling. The first is to get through to the right person. The second is to get an appointment.

If you don't know the name of the person, ask for the person's title. For example, if you're selling insurance, ask for the risk manager. If you sell office supplies, ask for the office manager.

If you don't get through, that is if you're connected to a secretary or voice mail, leave the right kind of message. It should be something that provokes a return call:

"Hi, this is Steve Schiffman, and I'm calling about the XYZ Corporation." (XYZ is a customer of yours and also one of your prospect's competitors.) Your message doesn't really have to mean anything specific. It's just something to get the conversation started.

If they get through, or when (not if) the prospect responds to their message, most people ramble on or try to sell instead of getting to the point of the call: to get an appointment. The idea is to start a conversation.

Another way to improve your ratio is to select potential prospects better. Prioritize those you call on first and concentrate on the most. By that, I mean if someone uses a product similar to yours and you can provide some improvement, that potential is great. If someone is located a three-hour drive away, you have to weigh just how much value there is in a sales call that essentially takes an entire day.

Here are some lessons to take away from this chapter:

1. Your sales volume can very likely improve if you improve your technique. You don't have to be a great or even motivated salesperson to get appointments. It's just a matter of technique to: get to the right person; leave the right message; and get an appointment.

2. Everyone does something well, and whatever it is—a sports activity, acting, managing—we tend to concentrate on it. Who doesn't want to do something he excels at? And this is true in the sales process also. But sales is a particular area where you have to concentrate on what you are *bad* at. Is making cold-calls a problem? Work on that technique. You have bad ratios? Improve them. Because if you don't, you'll never get to do the things you are really good at—whether it is mining for information, preparing presentations, or presenting them.

Chapter 4

Preparing for the First Appointment

You've made the call and got the appointment. Now what?

You prepare. You go to the Internet and look up every bit of information available on the company. You decide that it's important to go in knowing the prospect's company even better than the prospect does.

Then you rehearse your little speech. After all, the prospect is busy. You're lucky to get an appointment. So you want to make it quick.

I have three words to say about all of the above: Wrong. Wrong! WRONG!!!

Let's talk about research first. I know a salesman who spends an inordinate amount of time researching companies. He researches them to death, to find out if they are prospects, to find out who they are buying from now, to find out what their last quarterly statement indicated. And you know what the bottom line is? All that time is wasted because he has little success getting appointments. He ought to be concentrating on that aspect of the process instead of wasting time on research.

Besides, if you're even halfway decent as a salesperson, you already have sufficient knowledge about your industry to know who is a likely prospect, what they are currently buying, and from whom.

More to the point, no one likes a know-it-all. The goal of this initial meeting is to engage the prospect and to get him involved in your sales process, not to show off how much research you've done. The easiest way to engage anyone is to ask them questions about what they do—and listen to the answers.

Frankly, most people enjoy talking about themselves and their jobs. And it gives you an opportunity to show your interest.

But Steve, you say to me (go ahead, you can call me Steve), the prospect is busy. I can't waste her time asking questions. That's why I do the research.

No offense, but all I can say to that is boo-hoo. Get over it. First of all, everyone is busy. He's busy. She's busy. I'm busy. And you're busy. No one has enough hours in the day to do his or her job properly. E-mail, telephone calls, and visitors disrupt the day. You have to deal with it.

Beyond that, it's important—critical—for salespeople to remember that seeing vendors is part of the prospect's job. Seeing you is what the prospect gets paid for.

Your prospects are supposed to find the best possible deals and make the best possible arrangements for their companies. To do that, they have to see vendors. They have to be open to new ideas. They have to be aware that there are always other possibilities. You are doing your prospect a favor.

Yet time and again I see salespeople start off a meeting by apologizing for taking up a prospect's time, saying: "I know how busy you are. This will only take a few moments. I'll make it quick."

What's that I said before? Oh, yeah. . . . Wrong. Wrong! WRONG!!!

The prospect's job is to see you, and your job is to get to the next step. And that requires a positive attitude on your part, not an apologetic one. You are there to help him or her do whatever it is he or she does better than it was done previously. Be positive.

Remember, salespeople don't close a deal. They *coordinate* the deal. It is a collaborative effort that requires the participation and cooperation of the customer.

The purpose of this first appointment is to engage the prospect in conversation and determine whether she has an appetite for your product or service. You want to find out how the prospect does what she does so you can make it better.

So let me run you through a typical conversation when I make a sales call to give you an idea of what I mean:

"It's good to see you," I begin. "Nice weather. Before we start, would it be helpful if I told you a little about me and my company?"

"Of course."

"Have you seen any of my books out there?" I ask. I'll go on to describe some of my training programs, and then suggest, "We should talk a little bit about sales training. Just out of curiosity, do you run any sales training programs now?"

"We've done them a number of times."

"What kind are they?"

"The president of the company likes to bring in a magician who does his take on sales tricks everyone should know."

"Does it work?"

"No, but the president likes to do it."

"What are you trying to do?

"Get them out selling."

"My guess is that you have experienced salespeople who don't listen," I say. "They've hit a point in their careers where their lawns are more interesting than their jobs. I'd like to suggest something. I'd like to talk to a couple of your sales reps. Find out what obstacles they face. And based upon what I learn, come back to you with some suggestions about the kind of workshops I feel would be helpful for you."

I think it's pretty obvious what I did here:

- I engaged the prospect.
- I listened to him.
- I reacted to what he said.

But it all starts off by engaging the prospect, and the easiest way to do that is by asking questions. Most salespeople worry about coming up with the right questions. Don't worry about the questions. You know the questions. Worry about getting good answers. (If you insist on worrying about the questions, I suggest reading my book *Ask Questions, Win Sales*. And once again for the record, this is cross-selling, not shameless plugging.)

However, for those of you who cannot find it within your hearts to go out and buy that book, in the next chapter I will offer several examples of questions to ask.

For now, there are several lessons to take away:

1. Popular media have put salespeople in a category with politicians and lawyers. In other words, we're pond scum. That can lead to a certain amount of self-loathing. But if I may quote Tony Soprano, "Fuhgedaboutit." Salespeople perform not only a necessary function but a useful one as well. We bring newer, lower-cost, better-made products to the attention of consumers—whether those consumers are manufacturers, retailers, or individuals like you and me. So there's no reason to hang your head in shame or be tentative. The prospect's job is to see you. If he doesn't, he's not doing his job, and it is his loss.

2. You don't ever want to come to an appointment with a prospect or client and appear stupid or unprepared. But that doesn't mean you have to come to meetings with sheets and sheets of notes you found on Google, especially for an initial appointment. In fact, in all likelihood that's counterproductive. You want to engage your prospect in conversation and make her part of the process. If you come in to a meeting already knowing everything, what are you going to talk about?

3. If for some reason you do know everything, don't let the prospect know. No one likes a show-off. Give your prospect a chance to talk about herself and the company.

4. And when you get her to talk, listen. Don't worry about what you're going to say next. Be interested in the prospect's conversation—or at least fake it.

Chapter 5

Must You Question
Everything I Say?

I'm not a psychologist, so I can't tell you why, but people seem to respond to questions. What do you think? Is that your experience?

That's one of the reasons I frown on overresearching a subject. If you already know everything, what kind of questions are you going to ask? When you go into a first or early meeting with a prospect, there are three things you generally want to accomplish—and asking smart questions will do that for you.

Here are some points to remember:

#1: Sales Is a Process

I know, I know, I've said it before. And I will say it again. Often. That's how important this is. You want the prospect to agree to the next step. That step may be another meeting. It may be to arrange meetings with others in the company. Or in rare instances, it may lead directly to a presentation. But if you walk out of that meeting without an agreement to get to the next step, you've got nothing. Nothing.

#2: You Need to Gather Information

At some point along the line, you will have to make a presentation. At some point in the process, you will have to make a proposal. You cannot do that in a vacuum. Your proposal must be informed and targeted to your customer. You cannot do that without input from your client-to-be.

#3: You Want to Engage the Prospect

You want to get him involved in the sales process. You don't want the prospect to remain on the sidelines. You want him to assume part ownership of your sales effort. You want him on your team.

And to a lesser degree, you want the prospect to like you. Understand this: You are not friends. And you never will be. You may entertain him, take her out to lunch, treat him and his wife to a Bruce Springsteen concert. But you're not going to be friends.

That doesn't mean you can't have a good relationship. A good relationship is, well, good. But this is business, and a good relationship is beside the point. However, a bad relationship is not so good.

How do you gather information and engage the prospect? You ask questions. Intelligent questions. Intelligent questions that elicit long answers—like these, for example:

- What have you done in the past to handle a situation or problem like this?
- What made you decide to make this a priority right now?
- How do you maintain a competitive edge in an industry like this?
- What kind of new customers are you trying to attract?
- What's on the horizon for your company/department/team this month/quarter/year?

But there is more to this than just asking good questions. You have to listen to the answer and respond appropriately:

- Just out of curiosity, who else are you talking to?
- Why them?
- Have you ever bought a product/service like ours before?
- How did you make that decision?

In general, it's never a good idea to ask "Are you in charge of . . . ?" One reason is that a "no" answer to that question might lead exactly nowhere. (Also, your prospect might think she *should* be in charge of something but isn't—not a pleasant subject to bring up.) Instead, ask how a given decision was made the last time. Following the "how" will automatically lead you to the "who."

In fact, if you're ever stumped, you can't go wrong by starting questions with "how" and "why":

- How are you planning on making that happen?
- Why did you do it that way?
- How did you make that decision?

Here's another fits-all-situation series of questions:

- What are you doing *now*?
- What did you do in the *past*?
- What do you plan to do in the *future*?

And always remember that there has to be a method to your questioning. It isn't random. It is intended to help you get to the next step.

Instead of just summarizing the lessons to be learned from this chapter, how about some more questions? That's a good idea, don't you think?

1. What do *you* think the lessons of this chapter are?
2. What's the best way to engage someone in conversation?
3. If sales is a process, what are you trying to do in your initial meeting with a client?
4. What's the best way to do that?

Chapter 6

Some Rules for Questioning

In the last chapters, I discussed a couple of what I consider to be the key points of an initial meeting with prospects.

The first is that salespeople have to bring a positive attitude to the meeting. The prospect isn't doing you a favor by taking the meeting. He's doing his job. Do not apologize for being there.

Second is that the importance of research is often overstated. Any half-decent salesperson knows who the prospects are, what they do, and who they buy from. That's all you need to know going in. Your job is to sell, not show off your research abilities. The third key point is that you want to involve prospects in your process, and the best way to do that is by asking questions.

Simple, isn't it? Of course not. If it was really simple, we'd all be a lot more successful.

So here are a few more rules you should pay attention to. Early on in this book I suggested that the best way to plan the sales process is from the end. Consider where you want to go and work backwards from there to figure out how to reach your goal.

In the last chapter I gave you some specific questions to ask a prospect. Let me now suggest some general rules about the question game. They say that a good lawyer never asks a question to which he doesn't know the answer. It works the same way with you as a salesperson. When framing questions, consider what the answers might be. You don't want questions that can be answered with a simple yes or no. You also don't want to ask questions that can elicit an answer that may shut off further conversation.

For example, you could be left in an untenable position if you walk in and the first thing you ask is, "Are you happy with your current vendor?" or "What would you like to change about the service that you are currently receiving?" If the answer to the first question is yes and to the second is nothing, there's little room for you to maneuver. Typically, when salespeople get the wrong one-word answer, they immediately search for the nearest exit.

Try to ask questions likely to elicit answers that allow both of you some flexibility. That's sometimes easier said than done. If you're forced into a situation in which you have to ask yes-or-no kinds of questions, at least be prepared to follow up.

Just because the prospect says that yes, he is happy with a supplier, that doesn't mean you have to pack up your briefcase and leave. You could, for example, follow up and ask "How long have you been with them?" or "How did you pick that supplier?" The objective, obviously, is to keep the dialogue going in hopes of eventually finding some common ground.

"Look, I know you're not my customer. Let me ask you a question: Why not? Did we do something wrong?"

The response might be, "I had a rep come here a few years ago and he didn't listen to anything I said."

Your answer? "I apologize for that, and I hope you'll give us another chance. I guarantee that won't happen on my shift."

Or the response may be, "Frankly, we're getting the product a lot cheaper overseas."

"Well then, let me invite you to our factory. We're doing some very innovative things with our product; we have the most modern production line in the industry."

Another way to keep the conversation going: Don't ignore the obvious. My experience is that salespeople frequently take no notice of the 800-pound gorilla in the room. I'll give you an example from my own experience. I have an unusual phone system in my office. Don't ask me how I got it or why I got it, but it seemed like a good idea at the time. What I can't do with it is have two people pick up the same line in my private office.

What I had to do is get another private line, with one phone by me at the desk and another by the visitor's seat. This way, a visitor and I can both participate in the same phone conversation.

Believe it or not, I had a telephone system salesman come in, and he did not ask me about why I had this peculiar (even by my standards) arrangement.

Let us now assume you have a dialogue going. The best thing you can do is get others from the company involved in your process.

Did you notice that when I made my presentation, I suggested that I spend time with my prospect's sales reps to figure out what obstacles they face?

I call this process the Power of Twelve. I want to talk to twelve people in a company to get the best possible feel for what problems the firm is facing—at least in terms of what I sell. You can't always get a dozen; sometimes you'll only be able to talk to ten people. But the more you get, the better off you are, especially if you get some end users into that mix. This is such an important concept that Chapter 8 revisits it in detail.

For one thing, the more people you see, the more first-hand information you'll get that can be useful in your research. You can also build support for your products at various levels of the prospect's organization. Most important, the Power of Twelve gives you an excuse to come back and say "This is what I've found."

Getting to the Power of Twelve is relatively easy. "Now that you've seen my plant, I'd like to better understand your business. I'd like to spend some time with your engineers to see how they use the product."

You do this so you can clinch the sale, of course. But you do it because that is your job. In the same way that the prospect's job is to see vendors to discover new ideas and new or less expensive products for their companies, your job is to provide that information.

Sometimes the prospect will help bring in additional people of his or her own volition. For example, I once told a client that I thought I had a pretty good idea of what I wanted to show in a formal presentation, but I wanted to meet with him first.

"I'd like to walk you through an outline of what I've come with and have you fill in the blanks."

He responded, "Sure, but it would be helpful if I had a couple of other people here with me."

This happens all the time. It's not that people don't want to make decisions, they know that it's just smart to bring in experts in the field. If I sell steel, it makes sense for my prospect to bring in the people who will use the steel to these meetings.

It's once you've gotten this far that you can start to think about your presentation. But not yet. Before that, you have to sharpen your listening skills.

These are the lessons to be learned here:

1. The more information you get, the more likely it is that you'll be able to come up with a program that meets the needs of your clients.
2. The more people you see, the more points of view and info you'll get.
3. Don't overlook the obvious question. If you come into a room and you see a large pink elephant, you might want to ask what the elephant is doing there.
4. The more people you see, the more people you involve in the process and, consequently, the more people you'll potentially have on your side when decisions are made.
5. The Power of Twelve is not a show for the prospect to let him know how interested you are in getting his business. It's for you, which makes it doubly important that you listen to what people say. Really listen, not only to the facts, but to the subtext. Through the Power of Twelve, I've not only learned things that made for a stronger presentation and sales pitch, but I've also learned where the power resides. And it isn't always where you think it is.
6. It's always a good idea to verify the information you receive. Not everyone's perspective is the same.

Chapter 7

Ask, Listen, and Verify

I write this after having just returned from a sales trip to Europe. In London, the agent who represents me in Britain brought me along on a presentation to a prospective (and, it should be noted, potentially very large) client.

My experience has been that salespeople don't bring their bosses along unless they think it's a lock. They want to impress the head honcho, not depress him. So I was counting my chickens well before they hatched. I was actually thinking about how many frequent flyer miles I was going to rack up, about sitting on a spectacular beach on Kauai, about how I have to remember to get some really high-numbered sunscreen. (My secret is revealed. I too daydream about that a great success may be imminent, and I'm not immune to Hawaii's charms, either.)

But then the presentation began, and it soon became clear that the only island I was going to see was Manhattan—and that's because I'm based there.

The problem was that the agent gave a presentation based on what he thought was the best way we could help this company, not the best way the company thought we could help. When I asked him about it after the meeting, he hemmed and hawed a little. But in the end it turned out he'd based his entire presentation on a single thirty-minute visit with one executive at the company. And, almost always, that is not enough.

If you subtract the five to ten minutes of small talk that leads to a meaningful discussion, well, that doesn't really leave a lot of time. Which brings me back to (if you haven't already guessed it) a recurring theme in this book.

Your ultimate goal is to clinch a sale, and in order to do that, you have to convince your customers that you can help them do something better than they are doing now. It could be buying something more suited to their needs than a competitor's product, something cheaper, something easier to use. You have to make them willing to get off their, uh, executive chairs and change the status quo—that is, the way they've been doing business.

Everything in your presentation should be framed that way.

Let me give you an example of how that works. One of my clients is a business intelligence service. They do really excellent on-target surveys to determine why consumers purchase particular products. This, of course, is valuable information, and they have a number of high-powered clients, including a major software developer. It's something the company's salespeople trumpet whenever they make a presentation. In fact, that's all they do at meetings, talk about the work they did for this one client. But that's not helpful in their quest for new business. Other prospects have other needs and if you want to win them over you have to find out what they're interested in—not waste a lot of time talking about your past accomplishments. You need to gather enough accurate information about them to make intelligent choices about your next step. Then and only then do you even think about making a presentation. How do you get this info? As we've discussed before (and will likely discuss again), you ask questions and listen to answers.

This brings me to a pet peeve about listening. The prevailing wisdom is that salespeople should spend 90 percent of their time on a call listening and only 10 percent speaking. Poppycock.

I've said all along that selling is a collaborative process. The longer the sell cycle, the bigger the deal, and the more important it is that both companies—seller and buyer—work together. You need to find out information about the prospect and her company. She needs to find out about you and yours, as well. Can you deliver what you promise?

A good sales call is normally fifty-fifty in terms of speaking and listening. That's probably not what your sales manager is going to tell you. If you come back empty, he'll say you didn't listen. But listening isn't always the problem. Properly engaging the prospect is. And that means *not* doing the kind of listening salespeople normally do. My experience is that most salespeople only half-listen. That is, they hear what a prospect is saying, but they're not really paying attention. What they're really thinking about is what they plan to say next— regardless of what the prospect says. They're interested only in their message, and therefore they lose the opportunity to genuinely engage the prospect.

The irony is that listening is really the easiest part of the process for a salesperson. I was at a cocktail party the other day where I got into a casual conversation with a fellow guest. In twenty minutes I learned what his job was, how he got it, what he thinks of it, what other jobs he's held, and all about his family. I think that's typical of what most people do at a party.

Why not do that on a sales call? Salespeople need to create and master the flow of conversation. Unfortunately, salespeople on a call put on their sales face, take out a pad, and interview a prospect, often asking ridiculous questions, such as "Tell me something about your business."

That's the opposite of asking a silly question that calls for a specific yes-or-no answer. It's so general the prospect won't know where to begin. How about something like this: "Your Web site doesn't have a company history. How long have you been in business?"

Let us assume now that you've gotten the information you feel you need. For many, the impulse is to give a presentation on the spot, pull out the old flip chart or the new laptop, and run through what you have. Resist that impulse. Or if you don't, at least understand what you are doing is not a presentation but a demonstration. The two are different. If you do it here, it should be more to get a reaction than a sale.

Of course, there are very few hard-and-fast rules in sales. If you are convinced that you can make a sale then and there—and we all know that happens—you might transition into a mini-presentation by saying something like this:

"I've done some projects that are similar to yours. Let me show you the kinds of things we've done that might work for you." If it turns out the prospect isn't buying, that still offers you an opening. Ask what the prospect didn't like. You can ask for more information so you can tailor another less-generic presentation more directly to the company's needs. But understand this: The presentation you do at a first meeting will never be as strong, as persuasive, or as comprehensive as one that you could do later. Salespeople need to create and master the flow of conversation.

What you are better off doing is verifying the information you received. I'm not suggesting you regurgitate what you just said, but clarify and check key points. And you can use this as a way to get to the Power of Twelve. There's nothing wrong with telling the prospect, "I really want to understand the way you operate. The more I know, the better I'll be able to come up with a meaningful presentation. Are there some people on the line I ought to be talking to? Engineers? Your salespeople? I'll talk to as many people as I can."

There are several lessons to take away here:

1. The sales process is not about you or your company. It's about what you and your company can do to make the prospect's life easier, more profitable, or better in any other way. No one cares about you or your company except insofar as you can make the prospect happier.

2. You want to engage people in conversation—that is, a back-and-forth dialogue. You are in a business setting, and everyone knows that it is business being conducted here. But you can still engage people in conversation the way you would in a social setting. That way everyone is relaxed. Everyone is talking.

3. Don't jump ahead in the process unless you are absolutely certain you can make a sale. Otherwise, proceed slowly.

Part Two

Before the Presentation

Chapter 8

The Power of Twelve

Anyone who's been in the sales field for any length of time understands that there are no absolutes. For every rule I tell you, there's an exception. But if there's one thing that is even close to being an axiom, it is this:

Selling is not a race!

It's not an Olympic event. There are no medals for finishing the process first. The awards come if you finish the process *successfully*—that is, if you come back to the office with a signed contract.

If this were a race, frankly, the turtle would win every time. In sales, slow and steady always trumps speed.

It shouldn't surprise you, then, that one of my greatest frustrations is the willingness—nay, eagerness—salespeople always demonstrate to jump ahead in the process. They do it even though they're not ready to clinch the sale. More important, they do it even though the client isn't ready to sign on the dotted line.

More often than not, the step salespeople skip is the Power of Twelve. They seem to figure that the purchasing agent or the vice president of sales is as deep as they need to go into a company to gather the necessary data for a presentation.

That's wrong on a number of levels. The purchasing agent almost certainly doesn't have real-time in-the-field experience with the product you sell. Even the vice president of sales might not.

The closer you get to the trenches, the more useful information you're able to gather. The more people you see, the better the picture of the company you'll generally be able to draw. Certainly, the more people you see, the more allies you can make.

And, most important, the more sales opportunities you can unearth.

Consider this example, proof positive that Orson Welles was right when he said, "You shall make no presentation before its time"—or something like that.

Last year, I had an appointment with the CEO of a glass manufacturer. Pretty much all I knew was that it was a relatively small company (about $100 million in global sales) that made glass and had a sales staff of about fifteen people. I sat with him, made small talk and, as I always do, asked if there were a few people I might talk to so I could better understand what they do and develop a program for them.

The CEO suggested I speak to the vice presidents of domestic and international sales. I spoke to them at length and they led me on to a technical person. From there I went on a visit to a manufacturing facility, where I got the grand tour. There, I learned about a stand-alone product that was sold separately through a network of fifteen distributors and about 1,000 dealers.

This product wasn't on the Web site, and I wouldn't have known about it but for the Power of Twelve. With this knowledge, I was able to develop a sales training program that included not only the original fifteen salespeople I'd been shooting for when the process began, but the fifteen distributors *and* the 1,000 dealers.

That's what I'm talking about.

But there's still another reason for the Power of Twelve. When you involve someone in this process, when you ask them questions, when they have an opportunity to help you, they become *allies* in the process. They have partial ownership of your success. Especially if they are part of the team that listens to your presentation, they will root for you because they have a vested interest in your success. After all, they are part of your team. They gave you the information on which you based your presentation.

So please, do not underestimate the importance of the Power of Twelve. Handled properly, it can turn a cold call into a lasting and profitable relationship.

There are several lessons to take away from this chapter:

1. There is undoubtedly some point at which you have to stop talking to people and move on toward a presentation. But the truth of the matter is that I for one don't know where that point is. When people start telling me the same things I've heard from others, I'm tempted to cut short my Power of Twelve investigation. But if someone says to me, "You ought

to talk to Joe Smith in marketing," I'm there. Because I never know whether Joe is going to give me that one nugget I'll need to close the sale.

2. Whenever possible, go below the executive level to the end user. We all know that the people in the trenches know more and are more honest (given the opportunity) than their bosses ever will be.

3. I can't say this enough: More often than not, the people you interview, the ones who help in this process, become part of your team. In a small way, they have an interest in your success.

Chapter 9

Preparing for the Presentation

You've met with the prospect. That went really well. He loved your idea about checking with other people in the company. So you met with some engineers, a few people working on the assembly line, and then the prospect's boss. You are as ready as can be to proceed to the next step.

One of the first things you want to do to get set for a presentation is find out how many people will be listening to you. That number will largely determine the kind of presentation you do.

I break presentations down into three categories. There are those that match you with one or two other people. Then there are presentations at which you'll be addressing three to ten people. Finally, there are presentations for ten to twenty-five people.

A one-on-one or one-on-two presentation is usually a lot less formal and far more relaxed. You usually don't have to make a PowerPoint presentation.

Presentations for three to ten people almost always demand PowerPoint, plus the distribution of printed material. (Here's a note of caution: Do *not* hand out printed material until after the presentation; otherwise, people will be tempted to be flipping through it while you speak.)

Presentations to large groups, of course, always demand PowerPoint. In some cases, such as when your presentation involves a lot of numbers or other data, you should distribute printed material in advance. But understand that the larger the group, the more difficult it is to come up with an all-inclusive presentation. There are too many variables. The group will include people you've never met (perhaps the ultimate decision maker). These audience members may not know anything about your product and will not be as eager as some others to bring you into the company.

What do you do? When you find out how many people will be attending the meeting, also find out who they are. Assuming you've built a strong, positive relationship with the prospect, ask why these people have been chosen. If you feel comfortable doing so, see if you can determine what their agendas are. Do they know what the meeting is about? It's best if you can gain access to them. You can phrase this request like so: "Maybe I should give them a call and acquaint them with what I'm going to discuss."

The idea, of course, is to prepare them for the meeting and bring them up to speed with the people you've already spoken to. If you can do that, you avoid splitting the group in two. You don't want to go back and review everything that has already been discussed because that will bore people who've already gone through it with you. On the other hand, you don't want to go to a new start-up point and leave some people behind—especially if they're influential participants.

So you want to call them, and when you do, you should ask if you can send them some information. "By the way, did Joe tell you about me? No? Well, let me tell you very quickly because I think the program is very exciting."

If the answer is yes, you still shouldn't assume that the person really knows everything—or even anything—about what you've been working on. Ask if you can talk to her about something new that recently came up. You want to engage the person. If she is not involved, even on the periphery, she is less likely to feel any ownership of your ideas. Even if you just make an effort to contact these people, it's a step in the right direction. And the more you are able to engage them, the better off you will be.

Another factor in large group presentations is that you shouldn't make the presentation by yourself. The company has made a large investment in you by assigning so many people to your presentation. If for no other reason than psychology, you have to make an investment, too. At least three people—you and two others—should represent your company when a presentation involves ten or more people. The other people can't sit there like dolls. They have to take part in the presentation.

Having said all this, I should point out that group size isn't the only factor in determining what kind of presentation you make. The more complex your presentation, the more likely that you will need to use visual aids. If the presentation involves a lot of charts, for example, or numbers, you must have some form of visual aid. You might choose PowerPoint, overheads, or you might use a flip chart or white board drawings, the aids you choose will probably be determined by the number of people in the room. Remember, not everyone learns visually. But visual aids usually can't hurt, and they frequently help people understand your point.

The key, though, which is discussed in later chapters, is that you should not use visual aids just for the sake of using visual aids. Both words are operative. That is, you use visual aids to help you. If they don't serve that purpose—if they don't clarify a point you are trying to make, don't further your presentation—then they are a waste of time.

Finally, if you're running a presentation for just one or two people, you might very well walk away with a contract. But don't expect that to happen when you present to a lot of people. Depending upon the dynamics of that company, the people will have to get together afterwards and haggle among themselves. That's one of the great frustrations of these kinds of meetings. However, at the very least, you should leave that meeting with a firm action plan. Tell them you'll come in or be in touch the next day to answer any questions that they may have.

There are several lessons to take away from this chapter:

1. It's important to know who will be at the presentation—not only in terms of numbers, but in terms of their corporate responsibilities as well.
2. If these are people you spoke to in the Power of Twelve, you probably already have a pretty good idea of whether they're on board with you or not. If you don't know these people, it's not a bad idea to talk to your contact and find out who they are, why they are attending, and what role they'll have in the final decision-making process. Depending upon your relationship with your contact, you might also be able to find out where they stand in terms of the status quo—are they ready for a change, or will they defend the present supplier?
3. The medium is not the message. The message is the message. Don't worry about how you will deliver it—overheads,

PowerPoint, flip chart. The important thing is what you say, not how you say it. An attractive PowerPoint display that doesn't present any solutions will not clinch you a sale. A couple of flip-chart hand drawings that illustrate a well thought-out plan will do the job for you much more effectively.

4. Always remember to get the next step in the sales process— even at a presentation.

Chapter 10

To PowerPoint or Not to PowerPoint— That Is the Question

Even the most technophobic salesperson on the planet is likely familiar with PowerPoint. But there are still a few Luddites in the world who have yet to master this very important sales presentation software. If you are one of them—and I know you're out there—I beseech you to get off your computer-fearing seats and learn it.

When Is It Appropriate

Now, right up front I must admit that PowerPoint isn't the answer to every problem you have. But not knowing PowerPoint immediately creates an image problem for you. It labels you as old (no matter your chronological age) in a generation that values youth. It's like not having a cell phone or voice mail. People don't want to deal with a twentieth-century sales rep.

That doesn't mean PowerPoint is appropriate for all occasions. It does mean that you need to be familiar enough with it that you can whip out a presentation on short notice—there are situations when that is imperative. And you can't fake it. Even if you have a lot of help preparing the PowerPoint presentation, that can remain our little secret. You need to be able to talk intelligently about PowerPoint because a prospect may ask you a question whose answer depends upon your knowledge of the software. In short, your ability to press a button to move onto the next slide is no longer enough.

Advantage: Professionalism

First, here's the good news. The main advantage of using PowerPoint is that it gives you the patina of professionalism. You are hip, with it. If not a member of the MTV generation, you at least belong to VH1.

Another advantage is that you're not flipping charts or wasting time putting transparencies on a lit screen. It frees you to concentrate on your message and the reaction your words receive.

Disadvantages: Technical Difficulties

There is a downside to using PowerPoint, too. Computers crash. The screens and other equipment someone promised to have ready for you don't materialize. Or the extension cord isn't long enough to reach the outlet and your battery is dead. Welcome to the wonderful world of technology. Suddenly you're in a room full of hopefully eager potential customers with no place to go.

Besides technical failures, you also have to worry about your physical surroundings. If you do a one-on-one or one-on-two PowerPoint, you need to be sure that there's a place where you can put your computer so everyone can see it. If a prospect is sitting off at an angle or the lighting is wrong, he might not be able to see the screen properly and, as a result, won't get the full impact of the presentation.

I had a friend who ran into this problem a couple of times. She told me about a time when her laptop just couldn't find a proper home. Either one of two prospects attending the meeting couldn't see the screen or she couldn't. Because of the way the corner office was lit, the only way all three of them could view the screen at the same time was if they sat uncomfortably close.

My friend vowed from then on to use flip charts in one-on-one-type presentations. (Though as a precaution, she brings along her computer as a back-up, should the prospect prefer it.)

Know Your Environment

The same precautions have to be taken in presentations to large groups. I was at a recent presentation in a large room that was so brightly lit that people couldn't make out what was on the screen.

When the audience complained, the lights were turned down so low that it was impossible to take notes. (Of course, anyone who's been in sales for any length of time understands these no-win kinds of situations.)

I recently attended a presentation by reps of a large pharmaceutical company. There were several thousand people in a hotel ballroom. Obviously, in a situation like this, the primary requisite is that everyone be able to see. I say obviously but, believe it or not, I've been to presentations where people in the back didn't have a clear view of the screen.

That wasn't the case here. The rep had set up several strategically placed screens so that everyone could get a good close look at the pharmaceutical company's message—if indeed they were looking. But the room was dark and hot. Not warm. Hot. And the speaker droned on and on. I would bet that there were people in the back fast asleep.

Your first job is to ensure that everyone can see your work. If you are presenting in your room—that is, in your office or a meeting space you've rented—you have control. Get in there early. Be sure everything works and that the presentation is visible from every seat. Also check the temperature. You don't want it to be too cozy.

If you are meeting at a client's location, get access to the room well in advance of the scheduled start time. Check that everything you need is there and working. Allow time to fix anything that doesn't work.

If you're presenting with someone else—a sales manager, a coworker—both of you should bring laptops loaded with the presentation. That way if lightning strikes your computer, you have a backup.

You Still Have to Make a Great Presentation

While technical problems can certainly be vexing, they usually don't make or break a presentation. People understand that bad things happen to good computers. But they are less accepting of poorly thought-out presentations.

There was once a time in the years after PowerPoint presentations were widely used, that they were a novelty. You could throw pretty much anything up on the screen and people would oooh and ahhh. These days, people are pretty much numb to PowerPoint. The software can no longer carry your presentation. Your words have to.

What does that mean?

Don't Print Out Your Slides

You can't print out your presentation on slides. If you do, people will get your entire presentation just from reading it, and there's no reason that you should even show up.

Keep It Short

In fact, you don't want to have too many words on a slide, even if it isn't your entire presentation. A good slide has a simple phrase, a reference point on which you will expand with a meaningful statement of your own.

A former associate of mine has PowerPoint phrasing down to a science. He never uses more than a dozen distinct slides, but these slides allow him to cover everything. It works.

Beware Text-Heavy Slides

On the other hand, I was at a presentation given by a construction company I've worked with. The company used dozens and dozens of slides. But they didn't coordinate with what the presenter was saying. So his presentation raised more questions than it answered.

Understandably, people interrupted the presentation to ask questions, the answers to which were actually going to be covered ten slides down. As a result of all this back and forth, the construction company's sales reps never really got to finish their presentation in the time allotted to them.

Use Humor Sparingly

Another thing I've noticed is that people use little cartoon drawings in an attempt to make their presentation, uh, cute. It doesn't work. People smile at the cartoon and focus on the illustrated cow instead of your message. There's nothing wrong with using humor, but you have to be very careful. One person's joke is another person's insult. More on that later.

There are several lessons to be learned from this chapter:

1. Whether or not you use it regularly, it's important that you at least master the rudiments of PowerPoint. Failure to do so instantly labels you as a Luddite.
2. Using PowerPoint, on the other hand, gives you the patina of professionalism—if there are no technical glitches.
3. It's important to get to the meeting site early to ascertain that the room is set up properly, from lighting to electrical outlets.
4. Anticipate problems. Don't depend on PowerPoint to remind you of your presentation. You have to be ready to smoothly switch to a flip chart if a situation develops.
5. Don't translate your presentation to PowerPoint. PowerPoint should enhance your presentation, not be a substitute for it.

Chapter 11

The Guest List

You can do everything correctly. Prepare the prefect presentation. And then you run into a roadblock. Someone new gets invited to the meeting who doesn't like the way you part your hair or has a really good relationship with the status quo. You don't know the individual. She hasn't been involved in the process until then. Oops!

It would be really great for the salespeople of the world if we could pick the people who attend our presentations. Unfortunately, we have very little control over that.

That doesn't mean you have to blindly accept the list of attendees you're given, especially if you think certain people should be there who are not invited. I've had instances in which I've gone to a prospect and said, "When we do these kinds of things, we usually have someone from HR [or from IT, or you name the department] at the meeting. We find that very constructive in terms of the input and feedback HR [or IT, or you name the department] provides."

You have a bigger problem when you have too many people attending the presentation. There's no way you can ask to have someone eliminated. You can suggest people, but you can't exclude anyone.

Too many people at a presentation can only mess things up. In my experience, some of the people who come to presentations seem to have only one job—and that job is to come to presentations and ask stupid questions.

In those situations, try to address yourself to those people you know really matter. Frankly, it's difficult. If you don't know who they are, you may wind up ignoring and alienating someone important. But, on the other hand, you also have to be realistic. In the world of selling, there are gratuitous people who serve no other purpose than to send out negative vibes. Accept that and deal with it.

The truth of the matter is that the presentation guest list is one of the key points of demarcation in the sales process. The names on that list are an indication of your chances of moving on to the next step. Your ability to influence the list is perhaps the best indication of the relationship you have with the prospect. How does the prospect see you in the great scheme of things? Are you just an itinerant peddler carrying your bag of goods? If so, your authority (and likely your chances) is virtually nil.

On the other hand, maybe you've been able to convince the prospect that you are more than just a supplier, that you are a partner in his operation, that you share the company's vision and that you are a resource. If so, your odds of being successful (and influencing the presentation guest list) obviously increase dramatically. If the prospect wants to work with you, he will stack the deck in your favor.

But there are limits to what the prospect can do, no matter how good your relationship is. If a senior vice president wants to attend the meeting, the senior vice president will attend the meeting. And if the senior vice president has a bad attitude about you or your product . . . well, your job is to turn that baby around.

For the record, a person with a bad attitude (PWABA) is anyone who doesn't see the wisdom of buying your product. If the PWABA is someone you've already met with, someone who is part of your Power of Twelve, then you know what her objections are. You can address and overcome them during your presentation.

What happens if a PWABA you don't know turns up at the meeting? The reality is that this situation is difficult (and in many cases impossible) to overcome. When someone with a bad attitude is a last-minute invitee to your presentation—especially if that someone is a key player in the process—and that person walks into a presentation with a negative attitude, the reality is that you may not be able to turn that negative around. Part of the selling process is learning when to punt.

If you are getting a negative vibe, I recommend that you bring the issue up and argue against it. A sales rep I know was about midway through a presentation when he noticed that no one seemed to be paying attention. No one. So he brought it up:

"I'm getting the feeling that this is not resonating with you," he said.

He was right. His initial contact told him, "The reason is that we've already made the decision to go with someone else."

My friend was upset. When he told me this story, he put a positive spin on it. "At least it saved me all the agony of the rest of the presentation."

But what happened to him—and happens to all of us far more than it should—was terrible. I don't know why it happened. My friend is experienced, successful, and very much aware of the nuances of sales. This experience is atypical of what usually happens with him. He didn't have an inkling that anything was wrong. By all rights, the prospect should have felt he could tell him in advance. This would have saved my friend not only the agony of the presentation, but the money he spent on it and the time he put into preparing it.

Sadly, similar situations happen to the best of us. Even—and I know you're going to find this difficult to believe—me. I've given presentations where I thought I had a shot going in, but the questions I was being asked made it clear that my proposal didn't make as much sense to them as it did to me. So part way through, I said, "This doesn't seem to be of interest to you." A guy said "You're right," and the meeting ended.

There are ways to spot when you are losing individuals. That's the topic of Chapter 12.

Chapter 12

The Actor's Studio School of Presentations

I'm a big fan of Larry David and Christopher Guest. In case you are not familiar with their work, David was a creator of *Seinfeld*, one of the most—if not the most—successful and talked-about sitcoms ever on television. In his current project, he is head honcho of an HBO series called *Curb Your Enthusiasm*.

Christopher Guest (along with such talented collaborators as Eugene Levy) is the creative force behind a series of wildly innovative films, such as *Waiting for Guffman* and *A Mighty Wind*.

What these two people have in common, besides much of their comic sensibilities, is the way they work. As directors, both of them give their actors detailed background summaries of who their characters are, and they describe the situations that these characters find themselves in. What the actors don't get is a script. It keeps everyone on their toes and the projects fresh.

That's the way you ought to work when you make your presentations. You should internalize your message without scripting it, making it sound fresh and freeing you to go with the flow.

One of the worst mistakes salespeople can make is to come in with a one-size-fits-all presentation. No matter the prospect, no matter her company's needs, the sales rep goes with the same presentation. He has it memorized, and if anyone interrupts with a question, the rep loses his place.

It's important to remember that you are not the only person pitching your product, and your product isn't the only one the prospect is likely to be buying. In fact, depending upon his other responsibilities within the company, the prospect may see three, four, five, or more presentations in a typical week. Even if that is not the norm, if the company has just put out a request for proposals and is looking to close a big deal, the purchasing manager may decide to see bids from you and all your competitors.

In most cases, the purchasing manager or his committee will see through a rehearsed, scripted presentation—and by "see through," I mean "tune out." On the other hand, these same people will appreciate something that's fresh.

Obviously you can't go in cold. Using this approach doesn't mean you can't practice what you want to say. After all, you've done research. You know what the client's needs are. You have a good idea of who will be attending your presentation. So why not? You may be one of the lucky sales reps who is touched by a Higher Power, a sales rep for whom nothing ever goes wrong.

But the truth is that most of the time, the best laid plans somehow go astray. And that's when the power of the Larry David/Christopher Guest School of Presentations really kicks in. Because you've internalized everything and are not relying on a script, you can react to any unexpected changes. Good sales reps are able to move with the flow of the conversation.

A case in point is a presentation I recently gave in California. There were fifteen people in the room, and they kept interrupting me with questions. It didn't take me long to figure out that most of them didn't know as much about what we were doing there as I'd assumed. I'd provided everyone with an information packet, and I'd gone over some of this ground with almost all of them on the phone. But it was clear that they had dropped the ball in not preparing for the meeting, and I had dropped the ball in assuming that they would.

So I was faced with two choices. I could continue in the direction I'd been going with the presentation, based on my scrupulous research and my digging deeply into the Power of Twelve. Or I could be smart and change direction.

In this particular case, I did the smart thing. I went back to basics. I told them what I'd found out about their company in greater detail than I'd originally intended. I gave them more background about my company and what we do. Only then did I tell them what we could do for them. In short, I controlled the flow of the conversation and took back control of the presentation.

I can think of another example involving a company that sells legal information online. Reps from that company were making a presentation to a large law firm that was currently using a competitor. Typically, the legal information company presents to law firms' IT departments, and its reps talk about the software's functionality, specifically how easy it is to maintain.

But this presentation was attended by the firm's senior partners. While the legal information company began its presentation in the traditional way, its sales reps were smart enough to switch gears quickly. Instead of talking about the product, they talked about how lawyers use it, how easy it is to learn, and how swiftly the search engine works.

Here's another example. A real estate leasing company came in to make a major presentation to a major commercial account. The reps went into great detail about what the leasing company could do for the account in terms of research, negotiations, and delivery—all things they'd found important in their Power of Twelve research. The leasing company reps actually finished the presentation to a great round of applause. They had hired caterers to serve food afterwards, and they walked away that day thinking they had a contract all but signed up.

But they were wrong. When push came to shove, the company decided to stay with its current leasing company. What went wrong? The presentation was about the leasing company and what it had to offer and not about the account and what it needed.

Presentations typically must serve two masters. You are one master, and you have a message you want to get across. But the prospect is also a master who has a message she wants to hear. And your presentation has to serve both.

Some lessons to be learned from this chapter include these:

1. Presenting is in some ways like acting—unscripted acting.
2. If you walk into a presentation concentrating on a script you've memorized, you may miss important clues about how your audience is reacting.
3. Worse, you may be interrupted and not be able to find your way back to where you left off.
4. The best presentations are usually given by people who are able to go with the flow.

Chapter 13

Keeping the Business

It's one thing to get the business. It's quite another to keep it.

Someone I know had a conference with an existing client, a major account that produced several million dollars a year in revenue. The client was looking for new ways to use the rep's product, but when the rep went in to make his presentation he went in with a cocky attitude.

He assumed that the client was going to continue to buy from him because he was already embedded in the company. He assumed the client was content with the status quo. He assumed the business was his.

Of course, we all know what happens when you assume. Okay, for that one person who doesn't know (and because it cracks me up every time I say it), when you *assume*, you make an *ass* out of *u* and *me*.

The presentation this rep made was not fancy. It did not acknowledge that the client wanted to do business differently, and it did not vary in one iota from the presentation he had given when he first landed the account years ago. Believing incorrectly that nothing had changed within the corporation, the rep did not go in to search out the Power of Twelve again.

The reality is that if you already have the business and are called in to make a second presentation, you have a better chance of getting new business or retaining the old business than the person first coming in to pitch the account. You know the company. You know the people. You understand the nuances of the way they operate. You know the buzz words. Remember, too, that the status quo is a powerful thing. It's really hard to move an existing supplier.

But it is not impossible. Didn't you get the business that way from someone else? So don't get too cocky. It is important to remember that when a client wants to add a new product line or conduct a review of current suppliers, it is almost invariably because something has changed.

The change could be something as simple as budget cuts, and the company hopes to wring price concessions from you. But it could also mean personnel changes and internal politics, all of which you have to be aware of and stay on top of. So if you are asked to make a presentation at a company, it doesn't matter whether you already do business with it. You have to follow the same steps we've been talking about here. The first thing you have to do is find out what's going on.

I work with an advertising agency that had a large client put the account up for review. When I asked the folks at the agency why this was happening, they said it was all a normal part of some mysterious process. As far as they were concerned, it was a game that really didn't mean anything.

So the agency went on spending thousands of dollars—involving the salaries of some very high-paid creatives, mockups of print ads, and reels of television commercials—in the mistaken belief that nothing was wrong. When I checked into it (having been brought in after the agency lost the account), I discovered that the client had been unhappy with some results. The client was interested in moving in a new creative direction—but not necessarily in doing so with a new advertising agency. The agency lost the account because the executives there assumed the account review was all a game. They made no effort to figure out what, if anything, was wrong.

The truth of the matter is that a smart rep working for a smart company doesn't wait until the last minute to discover change. A smart rep stays on top of things—certainly at his largest accounts. I know I'm always checking in to be certain my clients are happy. And then you have to stay on top of the powers-that-be.

For example, at a very large company that we do business with globally, our number-one contact resigned. Obviously, I'm not going to go into too much detail about the company here, except to say it reacted in a way that large companies typically do.

The company immediately took away his Blackberry, his mobile phone, and his computer. The only reason I even found out that he was gone was that he had the courtesy to call me from his home phone. The only way I could reach him was to call him there or use his home e-mail.

I'd developed a good relationship with this executive, and when we spoke he told me what I needed to know about the politics at the company. We discussed who the new power brokers were and what plans they likely had in mind. He even suggested what I could do to keep the business.

We were just about to start a very large project with this company, and my old contact suggested I send an e-mail to the president of his division. I did, offering to visit his corporate headquarters to fill in the blanks on the project's status.

The key was whether or not he invited us to headquarters. If he did, it was likely he would buy into the project—and our presentation to him would turn the trick. If he didn't, then it was a whole new ballgame.

Another milestone came when someone was appointed to replace my contact. I'd like to say that the company had a hard time replacing him. He was smart, always looked out for the company's interests, and worked very, very hard. But the truth is that it's foolish to think that there wasn't someone else out there who was every bit as intelligent, as caring about the company, and as willing to put in long hours. And my job was to protect the business. As it turned out, my contact's replacement was a former assistant of his, a big supporter of ours and someone we'd known and cultivated for some time.

There are at least two lessons to be learned from this incident. The first is that nothing is permanent. Company goals change. Personnel change. And it's important to be on top of things. Too many salespeople I know sign a contract and move on to the next client. They pay only lip service to existing clients, because, mentally at least, the rep has already cashed that commission check and is worried about where the next one will come from.

One company we work with lost a contract with an exhibition company that they'd held for several years. When I looked into it, it turned out that no one had contacted the company in three years. Cocky. Complacent. Whatever you call it, it costs you business.

There's a second lesson here: Simply keeping in touch is not enough. Just because you already do business with a company doesn't mean you should stop efforts to build relationships with your customers. If we hadn't done that in the example I just gave, we might have lost that business. But because I had a good rapport with the man who left the company, he contacted me after he left. He told me how to keep the business. And, as an extra bonus, when he got another job, one of the first things he did was bring my company in to train his salespeople.

There's another hidden lesson here that is best illustrated by the following story, which recently made the rounds of the Internet. It is probably apocryphal. But even if it is, it serves its purpose here. Supposedly, it was written by a business student at a college who was surprised to find the following question on an exam:

"What is the first name of the woman who cleans the school?"

Surely this was some kind of joke, he thought. He had seen the cleaning woman several times. She was tall, dark-haired, and in her fifties, but how would he know her name?

The student handed in his paper, leaving the last question blank. Just before class ended, one student asked if the last question would really count toward the quiz grade.

"Absolutely," said the professor. "In your careers, you will meet many people. All are significant. They deserve your attention and care, even if all you do is smile and say 'Hello.'"

The student says that he's never forgotten that lesson—and he learned that the cleaning lady's name was Dorothy.

The point is that you can't just be nice to the top executives. I make it a point to know every secretary's name. There are times when I've had lunch catered, and I bring in enough food for the secretaries and people in cubicles near and far. If I have a piece of business, there is little likelihood that anyone will feel slighted by anything I do.

You always want to leave a group in a harmonious mood. You want everyone on the same page. If you don't, at some point in the future, you might run into someone who'll sabotage you because you made him feel slighted. Or he might have had a different agenda to begin with and you ignored him when you got the business and made no effort to win him over.

This is not rocket science. There's a certain amount of logic here.

Another lesson to be learned is to react right away. Yes, I was spurred on by my contact, but I immediately got in touch with the new power there and made an effort to get him into the loop.

I had a similar incident with another client. There was a major personnel change at the company, and the person taking over the department that controlled my budget was not someone I was particularly close to. Without any prompting, I got in touch with him immediately and asked if I could come out and make a presentation—even though I knew he was fully briefed on what we were doing.

I traveled out to California with members of my team, and we gave a presentation as though we were looking for the business for the first time. It was clear, distinct, and came with all the bells and whistles you'd expect. As luck would have it, the new guy decided to review the account. Because we'd been there, because we'd made the effort to see him, we were one of three finalists called back to make another presentation.

Based on our recent presentation experience when the new executive first took over, we knew who would be at the second presentation. We knew who would support us and who would not. As a result, we were able to put together a program that resulted in three of the committee members championing us.

We got the contract renewed. That would not have happened if we hadn't learned what the new decision maker wanted, if we just assumed we knew.

Did I tell you the story about what happens when you assume?

Besides those given above, here are some brief lessons to learn from this chapter:

1. An existing client is apt to stay with you if your contract comes up for renewal or review and give you additional business if the opportunity arises.
2. But don't take it for granted.
3. You have to treat existing clients as though they were prospects. Lavish them with attention and stay on top of changes, both in terms of personnel and corporate mission.
4. Remind yourself daily that nothing is permanent—especially your commission check.

Chapter 14

Ten Things You Need to Do Before a Presentation

There are a number of steps every salesperson should take before she steps into the room to make a presentation. Some of them are pretty obvious, but that doesn't mean that they aren't frequently overlooked. Here's the top-ten list:

> **Number ten:** Arrive early. Bring extra *charged* batteries for your laptop.
>
> **Number nine:** Make sure spelling and grammar are correct. Do you have any idea how stipid you loook if you mispel a word?
>
> **Number eight:** Walk around the room and make certain your presentation is visible and readable from every corner in the room. If not and you can, change the way the furniture is laid out so everyone can see everything.
>
> **Number seven:** Rehearse the presentation. And don't do it in front of friends. Rehearse it in front of the nastiest, most critical SOBs in your office. Encourage them to ask questions whenever they want. If you can survive that, the actual presentation will be a snap.
>
> **Number six:** If the aforementioned SOBs make some suggestions for improvements, listen. You don't have to make the changes. But sometimes you get so close to a project, you can't see the trees. Step away and look at the suggestions objectively— or at least as objectively as you can.
>
> **Number five:** Be sure you find out who the players are, and, if you can, their biases.
>
> **Number four:** Have a champion in the room, someone who will speak up for you.

Number three: Understand the vision of the company and the vision of your company—and know where they mesh—or where they can mesh, if they don't already.

Number two: Understand what the company hopes to accomplish with your product or service—and how you can help them achieve that goal.

And the number-one thing you should do before a presentation: Focus on the goal, your next step.

Part Three

In the Meeting Room

Chapter 15

The Parts of a Presentation

We all get letters and e-mails. I'm willing to bet that more than once, you've gotten a letter where the writer's point is buried somewhere in the fourth or fifth paragraph. People don't have time to get to the fourth or fifth paragraph. If they read the beginning of a letter and decide it's of no interest, there's a good chance they'll chuck it before they ever get to the point.

It's the same with a speech or a presentation. You have to get to the point quickly. Tell your audience why this presentation should interest them, capture their attention. It's not simple, and it requires a lot of thought.

One of the first things you have to do is to encapsulate what you are trying to accomplish. One of the theories I've heard is that you should be able to summarize your presentation in thirty seconds:

- "I believe that we can provide you with product X at a higher quality and lower cost than you are now paying and guarantee just-in-time delivery at no extra charge."
- "Our advertising agency has the pulse of the consumers, so we will better be able to create believable and effective marketing campaigns for you."
- "I believe our accounting firm can doctor your books much better than your present accountants—and we can even make it seem legal to the IRS."

Okay, maybe that last pitch was just there to see if you're still paying attention. But you get the point. It's only when you've been able to focus on your message that you can begin to sit down and write a presentation.

Remember, there are two parts to any presentation. The first part is what you want to tell your prospects. The second part is what they want to hear. A goods presentation includes both parts.

As with everything we've discussed in this book, you have to determine what the end game is, what the next step is in the process. Do you need to have another meeting? With a large group, you almost invariably will need some kind of follow-up. Or do you shoot to complete the deal right then and there?

Sitting down and writing a presentation can be difficult. However, my experience has shown that when I've successfully followed the process—that is, gathered the needed information, gone deep into the Power of Twelve—well, when I've done that, my mojo is really working and I breeze relatively easily through the most complicated presentation.

On the other hand, when I struggle, when I agonize, it almost invariably means I haven't done my homework. I don't really have a grasp of the situation, and I need to go back and redo parts of the process rather than make a presentation that is doomed to fail.

I know that no matter how much I preach about not doing canned presentations, some parts of any salesperson's pitch will be prepared ahead of time. If you give enough presentations, you start to sense what works and what doesn't. It's perfectly acceptable to use those things that work.

For example, you know your product or service. You know its strengths and its weaknesses. Logically, you probably discuss the strengths in every presentation, and you pretty much have that patter down. The temptation is just to use that. Don't succumb to that temptation.

Remember, the important point isn't how strong your product is. The key point is *why* that strength is important to your potential customer. How can she use it? Why should she care? The answer to that question is likely to be different for every prospect and therefore every presentation.

Starting Off Right

Another part of your presentation that might be canned is the very beginning. A presentation usually starts with a welcome, a short introduction of yourself and, if applicable, the colleagues accompanying you. Some people go around the room and ask people to introduce themselves. It depends on you, your product and service, and the types of companies you sell to. If you're presenting to a single corporate entity, these people probably already know who they are, and to ask them to introduce themselves may be considered frivolous and a waste of time.

The important thing in this first part of the presentation is that you insert something that creates a comfort level for you—and, if possible, your audience. I saw an interview with Paul Simon once in which he said that he plays the same song first at each of his concerts. I'm not a big Paul Simon fan. He mentioned the song, and it didn't ring a bell with me. But it's the message here that's important.

The tune is apparently an old favorite. The crowd likes it. It warms them up and gets them into Paul Simon. Just as important, both the song and the crowd's reaction to it warm Paul Simon up. This warm-up process gets him into the show.

Everyone should have a warmer-upper—something that creates a comfort level for you. I know I'm still nervous, and I've made probably thousands of presentations of various types over the years. So I imagine you probably are, too.

Here's what works for me. Right after the introduction, I talk about my background and experiences in sales, the number of sales I've made, and the various kinds of companies I've sold to. I illustrate how I have used the sales process that I will be talking about.

This does a couple of things. First of all, it warms me up. It's a part of my presentation that I'm comfortable speaking about. (There are some who know me who suggest that my comfort level is always high when I speak about myself. But I just ignore them. Where was I? Talking about my comfort level and speaking about myself.)

The other thing it does is let the audience know that I really am an expert, that I do this for a living.

Finally, it paves the way for me to get into the heart of what I want to discuss: the theory behind my sales process, how I developed it and how I put it into practice.

An associate of mine, a writer who runs a writing training program for corporate executives, always starts his presentation similarly, talking about the fact that he is a writer and brings that expertise to the course. He mentions the newspapers and magazines he writes for and then he holds up his latest book.

He follows that by saying, "Please, I ask everyone to put on your safety belts or at least hold onto your arm rests, because this next thing is really cool."

He then pulls out a Chinese translation of the book he just showed them.

This accomplishes a couple of things all at once. Everyone in the audience chuckles—and probably relaxes a little. My friend relaxes because when that first laugh comes on cue, it means he's on. At the same time, he establishes his bona fides. This isn't a guy who teaches because he can't do anything else. This is a man with impressive real-world experience. Most people haven't met any author, let alone one whose works have been translated. And he's done all this with a kind of self-mocking grin so he doesn't come off as a braggart.

The Reason You're There

In the second part of the presentation, after the introduction and your warm-up, you want to explain the topic you are going to discuss and why you think it is valid. As part of this process, you are verifying the information you received and on which you've based your presentation. For example, you might begin this section of the presentation by saying something like this:

"ABC Widgets is the premiere widget manufacturer in the United States—and has been for over 150 years. Your widgets were used on the transcontinental railroad, in the construction of the Brooklyn Bridge, and on every major domestic construction project. But you are now facing increased competition from cheaper widget imports that are making inroads domestically. Clearly, you don't want to lose market share. Over the next half hour or so, I'm going to tell you a little about how my company, XYZ Widget Supply Company, can help you."

Part three of a typical presentation is the rationale behind your thinking: How buying products from you is actually cheaper for ABC Widgets than buying from its current supplier; how just-in-time delivery can cut ABC's inventory costs; and how all this can be accomplished without any sacrifice in the quality of the finished product.

Part four has to do with details: pricing, the time table of when you can get started, discounts, and any other details you need to fill in. This is a good time to ask for questions. Usually what I do is question myself first. How am I going to be able to deliver all this? Can I really guarantee this price? That kind of sets the mood. Often in these presentations, people don't like to be the one to stand up and question anything. But if you're already doing it to yourself, it makes it easier for them.

Finally, the presentation should conclude with a thank you and some mention, if not resolution, of what the next step will be.

Take a Look at the View from the Audience

Here are two more basic but important tips. When you sit down to prepare your presentation, you want to write it as though you were going to listen to it. What that means is that you have to put yourself in the mindset of a customer.

I have noticed, for example, that salespeople sometimes gloss over important facts because they seem so obvious to the salesperson who deals with them every day. But what is obvious to you isn't always obvious to your customers. You are always safer assuming that there is someone in your audience who is not familiar with a particular fact.

Another advantage of looking at your presentation from the mindset of your customer is that it allows you to search for missing elements. If you ask yourself what else you would want to know if you were buying from yourself, you start to search for holes in your presentation. This lets you plug those holes up before your customers can point them out to you.

Remember the two-part presentation. You know what you want to say. Putting yourself in your customer's mindset forces you to think about what he wants to hear.

Tell a Story

Finally, as advanced as we are in the realm of communication, with books and television and satellite radio, we are still basically storytellers in the same way we have been since the Stone Age. Grandparents tell their grandchildren about what it was like when their mommy and daddy were young; we regale old friends with anecdotes of previous experiences; we tell stories to our spouses and partners reminding them about how we met and dated.

To the extent that it is possible, it is always better to frame your point in terms of a story. To illustrate that, here's a story that my writer friend of mine tells when he makes a presentation to a potential corporate client:

"When my son was a teenager, I took him in the backyard to build a picnic table. I did it for a couple of reasons. First of all and obviously, there was that whole father-son bonding thing. But also, I grew up in the Bronx. The most mechanical thing I ever did was to run down to get the building super to come up and fix whatever was broken. A picnic table is a kind of simple project. And I felt building one would give my son a familiarity with tools that I never had.

"So we built the table. It's upside down and we're screwing in the last screw. Then we take a nail and carve our names underneath, so that future generations will know who built this table. And then we turned it right-side up and it was just beautiful.

"But there was just one little problem. The only person we could invite to dinner was Shaquille O'Neal, because the table was up to here. (He brings his hand up to his forehead.) And if he came to dinner, he'd have to eat at a slant, because the table was also crooked. (He holds his hand out at a slant.)

"Why do I tell you this story? I had a carpenter come to my house, and based solely on my verbal description of what I wanted, without benefit of blueprints, he did a major expansion of my house. He had the carpentry gene. He was able to visualize and build what I merely described in (believe me) very layman terms. Obviously, I don't have that gene.

"But if I had taken a basic carpentry course, familiarized myself with the tools of carpentry, I should have been able to build something as simple as a picnic table. Well, it's the same thing with writing. Either you have the gene or not. I cannot teach anyone to write. But what I can do is familiarize your employees with some of the basic rules of writing, so that they're able to do relatively simple tasks like writing e-mails and memos with greater speed, quality, and confidence."

I really like my friend's approach. What he's done here is a couple of things. First of all, it's a cute story that always gets a laugh. Second, he's created realistic parameters. He isn't promising pie-in-the-sky goals that everyone knows he won't be able to deliver. And he gives assurances that what he can deliver is useful and will profit the company and its employees.

The power of stories is that you visualize it as it being told. When my friend told me this, I saw him and his son building the table and Shaquille O'Neal sitting there trying to eat dinner at a slant.

His story also raises another important issue. Ironically, when he started telling it—the story is true, by the way—the person who came to dinner was Kareem Abdul-Jabbar. But as his audiences got younger and younger over the years, fewer and fewer people knew who Abdul-Jabbar was—even though he was one of the greatest centers in the history of the NBA.

I said when you write this you should put yourself in the mindset of your prospects, that when preparing a presentation you want to think about what they want to hear. But you also want to consider your prospects from the vantage point of their demographics. If a group is made up mostly of women, perhaps sports references are less apropos than something else. (Please do not send me angry e-mails. I've considered that the previous sentence may not be politically correct. I also know that there are plenty of female sports fans—including many who know more about every game than I do. But we're dealing here with the law of averages.)

Similarly, if you are going to be addressing an older crowd, a reference to rap stars like Jay-Z or Eminem might not be understood. Please do not send even more angry e-mails on this point, as my inbox is already pretty full. I've considered that the previous sentence also may not be politically correct. Plenty of older folks know a lot about rap music. Personally, I know so little that I had to look up the names of those two rappers, and if I tried to reference them in my own presentations I might end up calling them Zee-J and Good 'N Plenty (who are not actual rappers, at least as far as I know). The point is this: Know your audience, and figure out what the greatest number of them will likely understand and relate to.

Clearly, a lot of thought has to go into each of your presentations—and the written portion is only one part of what you have to worry about. Here are some lessons to take with you as you go into the meeting room:

1. Get to the point! The best way to write a presentation is to start by summarizing what it is you're trying to say in one sentence. It's a lot easier writing a presentation once you are able to encapsulate your message.

2. Every presentation has two parts: the message you are trying to get across, and the message your prospects want to hear. It's important to keep that in mind when writing. Don't just explain why your product is great; explain why your great product is good for the company you want it to sell to.

3. Don't gloss over facts because you think they're obvious. What is obvious to you may not be to your audience.

4. Be a storyteller. Illustrate your points with stories—for instance, tales of how other companies have used your products.

5. When preparing your presentation, always keep your endgame in mind: What is the next step? Do you want a commitment, another meeting, feedback? That's what your presentation should lead to and conclude with.

Chapter 16

Building Rapport

You are about to enter a large room with a group made up of mostly strangers who hold at least a portion of your future in their hands.

Ideally, you know or at least have met everyone in the room. In the real world, though, you probably don't.

Ideally, you know who is on your side and you know who isn't. In the real world, though, you probably don't.

Ideally, they all know you or at least know about you, and they are in this meeting because they genuinely want to hear what you have to say. In the real world . . . well, I don't have to tell you.

The bottom line: You only have one chance to make a first impression.

I've said repeatedly that sales is a process. But it works on two levels. The first is the obvious one that we've been talking about over the last dozen or more chapters. You go in for a meeting to introduce yourself and learn about a prospect's company. You know how your prospect can help you—by signing a contract and awarding you the business. But you have to know how you can help her, so you meet with, say, the purchasing manager.

If you work it right, you meet end users, company executives, maybe even the CEO. They provide you with the information you need, and you prepare a presentation that will dazzle them.

One step leads to the next and, while any misstep can derail the entire effort, it's a simple and logical process that makes sense. Sure, you're not going to get the sale every time, but if you don't there's generally a reason for it. You didn't have the right product or service. The price was not right. You couldn't guarantee delivery dates.

But then there's the other level, the one that's more subtle. Someone who is important may just not like the cut of your jib. You unintentionally send off bad vibes.

Most of us know that there are a lot of ways people communicate nonverbally. They do it with posture. They do it with their clothing.

And each of these things, wittingly or not, tells a little something about ourselves to the people around us.

Dress the Part

Motorcycle gang members dress like motorcycle gang members. And believe me, I'm the last person who wants to disrespect a motorcycle gang member, mostly because I'm a well-known coward. But I know several police officers who are members of motorcycle clubs, and when they go out for a weekend spin, they dress in a manner typical of motorcycle gang members.

If you saw them coming down the street, you'd swiftly hide the women and children. You quake even though they are cops because they give a different impression. Well, it's the same thing in sales. If you look or act like a gang member, people will react to you as though you were a gang member. At that point, your message becomes unimportant—because no one is listening.

I'm confident that most of you know and do everything I'm about to suggest here. But for the record, let me touch every base, dot every "i" and cross every "t" because, frankly, it took me a while to catch on to how important this was.

It starts with your appearance. When I was a young salesman and money was tight, I bought my suits off the rack at a discounter. They were fine suits, available elsewhere (as the retailer advertised) for several hundred dollars more.

The suits were fine. They fit okay. I looked okay. And I did okay. But I made it a point to go out and buy one expensive and tailored suit that I wore only when I was looking to close a sale. I called it my presentation suit. It fit perfectly. It made me seem invincible. Not only did I look good—good? I looked *great*—from the outside looking in, I looked good from the inside looking out.

By that, I mean people complimented me when I showed up for presentations. Truth be told, they were probably complimenting my presentation suit, but I graciously accepted it as a compliment to me.

More important, the compliments (and my suit) bolstered my confidence and self-esteem. I felt as though I could do anything, and so I did. I know it sounds a little corny, but I was this young punk, not long out of school, and all of a sudden I found myself in a pond with a lot of big fish—some of them sharks. But I survived. Heck, I thrived. Looking back, I can honestly say one of the reasons for my success back then was my presentation suit. Joseph may have had his Technicolor dream coat—but I always felt I had something better.

A friend of mine teaches communications skills to executives. When he first started out years ago, he had a chance to deliver a pilot program. That is, he delivered a version of his course to people from the training department who then rated him. That rating would determine if he got a contract.

He didn't. And while it may sound silly, the reason he didn't get the business was because he wore a brown tweed suit and brown shoes. Yes, this was a number of years ago when there was a greater formality in business, but (and my friend later saw the evaluations) my friend was rated unsuitable for this bank even though most of the folks rated his course highly. When push came to shove, he didn't wear the dark suit, white shirt, and blue tie that the bankers expected of him.

This wasn't his first meeting with executives at the bank. But the other sessions were less formal. He met one-on-one most times, and maybe it was the force of his personality that prevailed on the human resources person (it was simply the personnel department back then) to overlook his improper dress. Maybe they assumed that he'd put on the corporate uniform when he delivered the pilot program. Maybe because they got to know him, they were embarrassed to mention something that they probably realized was trivial.

And as for my clueless buddy, he was very young at the time. He just thought a suit was a suit.

Times have changed, but the principle hasn't.

I believe that part of the process of creating rapport is looking the part. You're not a calypso singer. You are a professional, and you should dress like one. Look at the army and navy. There's a reason a general looks like a general while a private looks like a private.

There are some people who say you should match the style of the company when it comes to dress. I disagree. I recently presented to a high-tech company, and everyone there, including the company president, came dressed in a polo shirt. But it didn't take me long to figure out that all those shirts bore the company's logo. That was their uniform. Your uniform is a suit.

Talk the Talk

Building rapport involves more than just clothing; there are cultural issues, as well. I made a presentation in New York to a foreign-owned company. Everyone there spoke English. But the presentation didn't go well because the people there didn't want to work with me in English. They had their own agenda, and frankly I should have picked up on it well before the presentation. But I didn't. Had I done so, I probably would have prepared handouts in Italian, their language. While I would still have made the presentation in English, that gesture might have been enough to get them to work with me.

That's certainly what happened on a trip to Japan. Perhaps because the culture is so radically different from what I'm used to, I made a special effort to read up about it. I had cards printed up in Japanese as well as some of the handouts. Because I made the effort, my prospects went out of their way to accommodate me.

The bottom line is that because we are becoming much more global in our commerce, it behooves us as salespeople to become more global in our thinking. The country is becoming more diverse, too. I have an Italian contractor remodeling a vacation home I own who has learned Spanish so he can better communicate with his workers.

I'm not suggesting that you go to foreign-language school. But it is important that you learn the customs of your customers. I have a customer who is Indian, and he has a different expectation of the way a meeting should go. Often, decision-makers from foreign-owned companies are here on temporary assignment. While many try to blend in and become sensitive to the American way of doing things, quite a few do not. It becomes your responsibility (assuming, of course, that you want to make a sale), of doing it the customer's way.

Incidentally, this is not just true for foreign or foreign-owned companies. Although this seems to be becoming less prevalent than it once was, there are (or were) pronounced regional differences in the way meetings are conducted in this country, too. In the South, for example, there's traditionally been more small talk before presentations begin than in the Northeast.

The problem, of course, is that while dressing appropriately or being sensitive to cultural differences probably isn't enough on its own to get you the business, not doing so can kill you. Continuing to build rapport during a presentation is the subject of the next chapter. Here are a few things to remember from this one:

1. You only have one chance to make a good first impression.
2. To quote Fernando, the Billy Crystal character from *Saturday Night Live*: "It's better to look good than feel good." For better or worse, you're often judged on your appearance. The better you dress, the better you will be perceived.
3. Looking good won't win you a sale, but looking slovenly might lose you one.
4. In an age of globalization, it's important that you be aware of cultural and language differences. Behavior that may be acceptable in the United States might be considered scandalous to someone raised elsewhere.

Chapter 17

A Few Words on Maintaining Rapport

The friend of mine whom I mentioned in the last chapter, the one I'll call Brown Suit Guy, teaches a business-writing course. The course lasts two days. Of the roughly sixteen hours he spends with his students, he allots just ten minutes to grammar. His classes are typically made up of middle managers and higher-ups, often MBAs. He coaches senior executives on a one-on-one basis. Almost everyone in his classes has at least a college education.

His rationale is that if his students haven't mastered the basics of grammar in twenty years of education, if they don't know that every sentence needs a subject and verb at this point in their lives, well, it's too late. He argues that it's better to spend the limited time he has with the students practicing writing skills. I feel the same way writing or speaking about maintaining rapport.

I've long felt that by definition, salespeople are folks who know how to interact with customers. They are naturally gregarious, the kinds of people that other people want to be with. But every time I get completely comfortable with that notion, I hear a story that literally shakes the foundation of my basic beliefs about this business.

A salesman (and I've never known a woman to do this) tells an off-color or insensitive joke at a presentation. Someone gets drunk at lunch just before showtime. Someone shows up completely unprepared.

You'd never do that. Of course you wouldn't! You understand that the easiest way to build rapport is to be sincere, to be genuinely interested in the people, to be genuinely interested in the company, and to believe in the benefits you can bring to it.

"Sincerity is the key, and once you can fake that, there's no limit to your success." I'm not sure who said that, but it's true. The reality is that people aren't going to buy your product or service because they like you. But they may *not* buy because they don't.

At least when it comes to grammar, you can teach that. I think the ability to project sincerity is inborn. But there are tricks that can win people over even if you were not blessed with the sincerity gene.

Brown Suit Guy has one of my favorites. He gathers everyone before he starts his presentation for a group picture. He has someone hold a hand-lettered sign that says "Before" and asks everyone to pose as though they were angry. "Gangsta angry," he says, "because you don't know the details of my writing course."

At the end of his presentation, he gathers them again, only this time the sign says "After," and he gives them permission to smile.

Then, depending upon how quickly a decision will be made, he sends everyone at the presentation copies of the photos—either via e-mail or snail mail. He includes a note that says "Look at how sad you look before you knew about all my writing course has to offer. And now look at how much better you feel once you found out about it."

It's a hokey thing, but he claims it always works. He doesn't always get the contract, but people leave the presentation with smiles on their faces, positive attitudes in their hearts, and a predisposition to like him—brown suit and all.

That's not the only one.

Chapter 18

Nonverbal Responses

I was in the middle of a presentation once when I looked up and noticed three women sitting in front of me with their arms crossed sharply in front of them. We all know (or soon will, after finishing this chapter) that there are a number of nonverbal clues to how people feel.

Without going into too much psychological mumbo-jumbo, if you are speaking and you see people with crossed arms in front of them, as a general rule this is not a good thing. It means they are closing themselves off. They are not interested in what you are saying.

Or, as in this case, it means they are sitting under an air-conditioning duct and are freezing. The lesson here is that you have to be careful in evaluating nonverbal clues and how you respond to them. They are often deceiving.

For example, if someone pinches the bridge of his nose, usually with eyes closed, this is supposed to be a sign that the person is in deep thought, deliberating presumably about your presentation. The prevailing wisdom is that you should wait to hear what he has to say to find out what their objections or doubts are.

But what if the only thing he's thinking about is whether he should interrupt the presentation to go get some aspirin because his head is really killing him?

Another one of my favorites is the guy who rubs his ear or just behind his ear with his index finger. Even when done subtly, this is supposed to indicate doubt, as in, "I don't know if I agree with you."

Or it could just that be his ear itches.

The problem in reading nonverbal signals, of course, is determining how to react to them. That really depends on the size of the group. Sometimes you can't.

If you are addressing a large group, people who send out negative vibes are nothing but unintentional hecklers. They aren't necessarily mean. And in most cases they don't intend to do it. But crossing your

arms in the middle of a presentation—and in sight of the presenter—
is really no different than talking in a night club in the middle of
someone's act.

I've seen professionals, well-known and well-regarded singers, get
flustered when that happens. Even comics who are supposed to be
able to handle hecklers occasionally lose their cool. So what are you
supposed to do without years of entertainment-industry experience?

The most important thing to remember is that just as you have
little experience in reacting to hecklers, you probably also have little
experience in reading body signs. So you may just be wrong.

The natural inclination is to address the person or persons
expressing negative feelings, to play to them. But what can you do?
Can you interrupt the flow of your presentation to say, "Excuse me,
sir, but you've adopted a very negative posture, and I'm wondering if
there's something I can say or do"? Of course not.

If possible, depending upon the layout of the room, one of the
things I try to do is stand next to or near the heckler. I've found that
sometimes this gets the person off her negative track and sometimes
gets her involved in other (hopefully more positive) aspects of my
presentation.

If you periodically stop your presentation to ask if there are any
questions, you might do that while you're standing in front of the
person you believe is expressing negative vibes. But you only want to
do that if you believe you know what his objections are—and if you
have a good response to them.

True story. My son-in-law was at a presentation of a coalition of
companies that do business with the federal government. There were
300 people in the audience, and the gentleman giving the presentation typically got people in the audience up from their seats, brought
them up front, and made them part of the presentation. I'm guessing
he looked for people who were less than interested in what was going
on. I say that because he seemed focused on a woman whose back
was turned to him and who didn't seem to be paying attention.

He called her up, but there was a slight delay while she gathered
her things—including a seeing-eye dog. She was blind and had no
reason to be looking at him. The presenter seemed taken aback for
a second, but then he did the smart thing and continued as though
the woman was sighted. She didn't seem offended, and the audience,

which was also taken a little by surprise, seemed relieved that everything went smoothly.

The story illustrates two important points. First, appearances can be deceiving, especially when it comes to body language. Second, you can't script a presentation. You have to be prepared to think quickly and react to situations you didn't plan. Situations you never thought would take place in your wildest dreams. In this case, everything worked out. The presenter had the presence of mind to continue—the proper decision under the circumstances.

Under most circumstances, however, the best thing you can do when making a large-group presentation is to try to ignore the person, continue with it, and hope your argument sways the remaining members of the audience.

But that's less true when presenting to smaller groups of, say, three or four people. In that situation, you normally have more give and take. What follows are some common verbal gestures and suggestions on how best to respond to them. Please note that these gestures and signs can also come during earlier meetings and not just presentations. Your response to them would be the same.

Facial and Neck Gestures

Raised eyebrows: This typically is an expression of astonishment or disbelief. It is often accompanied by an exaggerated opening of the eyes or flared nostrils. It's not necessarily negative. In fact, it could mean that your point has been made and the prospect is agreeing with you. Depending upon the group and the point you have reached in your presentation, you might follow up with something like, "I know it sounds too good to be true, but I have all the facts and figures to back me up."

Licking the lips: This is usually a sign that the person you're speaking to is fibbing, misleading you, or stretching the truth. It's a good idea to ask questions to try to confirm your suspicions.

Pinching the bridge of the nose: This is usually accompanied by closed eyes. Indicates a deep conflict (or, as noted previously, a migraine). Attempt to find the reason for the disagreement, and attempt to resolve it (or get the man a Tylenol).

Backward head tilt: This is another indication that something has displeased the person. Attempt to engage the person, if possible, and address the problem(s).

Lip-in gesture: This is a sign of doubt or uncertainty. Ask questions to obtain additional information and respond accordingly.

Beady-eyed: This is a clear signal that the person is serious and all-business. If possible, do not break eye contact with her. This shows that you are also serious about the issue at hand. This of course is easier if this is a one-on-one meeting. Obviously you cannot exclude the others present just to keep eye contact with Ms. Beady, but do return to her regularly.

Avoiding direct eye contact: This person is trying to hide from the current situation or question. Remember how you used to do it in school when you didn't know the answer, and you figured if you looked down the teacher would never call on you? This is the same thing. You're being shut out. Ask questions to find out if there's a problem or, worse, if a lie is somehow part of the discussion. Remember, getting false information or feedback is as bad or perhaps even worse then getting no info at all.

Strong eye contact: This person is thoroughly engaged in what you are saying. Capitalize on this person's interest; get him more involved in the presentation.

Eye movement to the left or the right: More often than not indicates truthfulness or forthrightness. It is a sign that a person is digging deep to respond to or make a statement about the subject currently being discussed. After she does, follow up accordingly.

Compressed lips: Suggests that person is facing some type of inner turmoil. This could interfere with your sales effort. There is clear conflict to resolve. Depending upon the scenario, try to calm the person or diffuse the situation.

Hand Gestures

Open hands turned up: This is the opposite of licking the lips. The gesture says this person has nothing to hide. This person is being honest and sincere, and there is a high degree of likelihood that you can trust what she says.

The nose touch or rub: This is a very strong indication that the person is being dishonest. The gesture may be subtle and will often be accompanied by other movements, such as squirming in the chair or physically withdrawing. It's important to ask follow-up questions and figure out what's going on before this person leads you down the wrong path. It's very important to verify whatever information the nose-rubber gives you.

Steepling: When a person puts fingertips together to form a steeple, he is very sure about himself and what he's saying—to the point of cockiness and perhaps even egotism. Give this person his head; unless absolutely necessary, do not disagree with him.

Fingers to cheek: This person is processing what is being said or explained. She is likely to be working out an issue. Follow up by asking a question or for a response or comment.

Closed hand or fist: A sign of disagreement, turmoil, or anger. Try to conciliate. Make a mental note that your comments have created resistance in this person.

Hands on the back of neck: This position is assumed by people who feel superior in knowledge or position at the moment. It is a gesture of relaxed aggressiveness, most common in males. Some people believe you need to neutralize the person by standing up or displaying a sign of authority yourself. But that's only if you have authority. If you're selling and this person is the one who signs on the bottom line, standing up to him may only cause him to become more aggressive and more negative in his feelings.

Eye rub: This is often a sign of doubt. It is entirely proper to ask questions that seek to identify the nature of the resistance or disagreement. Depending upon the situation, it is appropriate to ask, "Is there a problem? I sense a little hesitancy on your part."

Brush off: Another indication that the prospect doesn't accept your point or points. Again, it's suitable to ask if there is a problem.

Hips, Legs, and Feet Gestures

Arms and legs crossed: This indicates defensiveness and is another instance in which it is appropriate to ask "Is there something wrong? I sense resistance" or "Do you disagree?" It's another one of those can't-lose situations. If there's nothing wrong, you haven't lost anything. But if there is a negative feeling there, you may be able to turn it around and keep it from festering.

Legs open: This gesture reveals openness and receptiveness to your message. This positive reaction indicates you should continue along the same path.

Knees together with ankles crossed: This person may be trying to hide specific information or may be opposed to what is being said. The operative word here is *may*. Watch to see if there are displays of any other resistance signs. If so, you may need to defuse the situation or ask additional questions.

Leaning back in chair: This is a gesture commonly associated with a negative reaction to an issue. This person is hesitant and not buying what you're selling. Ask questions to try to determine what led to this resistance and to see if there's some way you can try to turn it around.

Legs twisted: This person is uncomfortable in the present situation. If it's about a question you've asked, try to ask the same question in a different way. If it's about a statement, rephrase it to check the validity of the person's nervousness.

All of these nonverbal signals need to be weighed against a certain amount of common sense. If a person is showing a negative nonverbal gesture, do you automatically react? Not necessarily.

Your reaction depends on a number of factors. What is the vibe of the room? If you feel you're getting through to everyone else, there's probably little point in singling out one person with a negative view. If this is a one-on-one presentation, then you have little choice but to attempt to root out negative feelings.

What About *Your* Nonverbal Language?

While you are busy scanning your audience for nonverbal clues, your prospects are looking at you, too. It's not something overt. It's not like they consciously say, let me look at his or her posture to read what it says. But it's there and if you deliver a presentation with your arms crossed in front of you, your prospects will know. And those that don't know will sense it.

The easiest thing to do is consciously always present in an open posture. Easier still is to always walk into a room with a positive attitude. You have to tell yourself it's all over but the presentation—the contract is yours. There is nothing that can go wrong. And if you believe that, your nonverbal language will reflect it.

Some lessons to keep here:

1. You can't just pay attention to what people say. What they don't say matters, too. And that is often expressed by their body language.
2. You want to pay attention to nonverbal signals. But use them only as a guide. Unless you're a trained psychologist, you might just be misinterpreting body language.
3. You can't let negative body language fluster you any more than you should let negative comments fluster you. You may have to modify your presentation to take into account an unexpected reaction, but don't let it throw you for a loop.
4. You're giving off body signals, too. Be sure you always maintain a positive posture.

Chapter 19

Using Humor

All of us go to industry conventions. We meet people. We hand out business cards. We collect business cards. And in the post-conference haze, most of us forget who we met and why those people may or may not be important to our professional lives. But, no matter. We love them all and send each and every one of them a letter saying so: How nice it was to meet you; let's do this again; and by the way, I sell widgets, should you need any.

I know a salesman who is very funny. He cracks me up in normal conversation. He tells jokes really well. And he knows how to network. He decided a few years ago to set this practice on its ear. Here is the "personal" letter he sent to everyone whose business card he collected. Literally.

> Hi, [insert name here]:
> It was a pleasure meeting you, meeting you, meeting you at the conference, conference, conference. As you know, know, know, a lot of people come back, come back, come back from a convention, and have their secretaries feed feed feed a form letter form letter into a computer, computer. They spit out these personal letters letters letters. And then they don't even bother to proofread them, proofread them, proofread them. But of course, I'm not like that, not like that, not like that. This letter is sincere, sincere, sincere.
>
> Regards,

Over the years that my friend sent this letter out, he got an overwhelmingly favorable response from its recipients. People remembered him because of it. The next time they saw him, they often made a point to come over and say how much they loved it. One person he'd sent it to—a very high-level executive—asked for another copy. He'd misplaced the original in the process of showing it around and getting appreciative laughs from his colleagues.

I'm pretty sure you know where this is going. Sure enough, at one point, someone was offended by the letter. The offendee was close to my friend's boss. The offendee called my friend's boss to complain about how offended he was. The offendee believed the letter was immature and unworthy of the company. It was a disgrace.

Before I go much further, let me assure you that there were no repercussions for my friend. He was closer to his boss than the offendee, but it does serve as an example of the dangers of using humor.

The reality is that professional comedians, who supposedly know what is funny, are known to bomb. And the chances are you are not even a semi-pro in the field. So let's look at a couple of plusses and minuses of using humor.

The biggest plus, of course, is that comedy loosens a crowd up. People sitting in on your presentation may be bored, tired, or disinterested, or they may be suffering any number of other pro-fessional maladies. Get them to laugh, and the clouds disappear. People wake up and pay attention. That's why good speakers often start speeches with a joke.

But you have to be careful about a couple of things. As noted, the fact that you think a joke is funny doesn't necessarily mean everyone in your audience will laugh. Another friend—make that acquain-tance—of mine started a presentation with a joke that was so off-color I was embarrassed. And if you knew me, you'd know very little embarrasses me.

This gentleman (and for some reason it's almost always guys who tell the wrong jokes at presentations—and elsewhere for that matter) happened to have given a really good presentation. Under other circumstances, I bet he would have gotten a sale. But at the end of the day, the talk wasn't about his product. The talk was about the risqué presentation.

But it's not just about being risqué. Sometimes it's just about being able to tell a joke well. And yes, you know who you are (or at least should). Some of those smiles you are getting are not from people who appreciate your humor—it's just pity. As with everything else in terms of presentations, you have to go with your strengths.

Another important point is that even when a joke is funny, it doesn't necessarily add to your presentation. The issue is style and substance. Is the joke somehow on topic? Does it further the message you want to get across? If not, the joke can serve as a distraction.

All this goes beyond just the oral part of your presentation; the same wisdom applies when it comes to using humor in your PowerPoint slides. Consider this slide, for example.

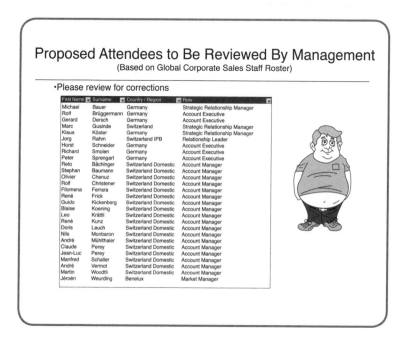

It is bad on many levels. The font size is too small. Most people won't be able to make out the names on the list. There is too much text. To make sense of this slide, you have to really spend fifteen or twenty minutes on it, which is much too long. Moreover, while the cartoon may be a momentary distraction from an obviously bad slide, it doesn't make the slide any better or even palatable. So it serves no purpose.

Finally, in one of my classes, one of the students gave a very funny practice presentation. He was very stylish, very engaging. But when the class evaluated him they talked about his wonderful sense of humor and how enjoyable the presentation was. No one mentioned the product he was supposedly selling.

I'm loath to say you should avoid using humor. But I do suggest that you use it only to emphasize and further the points you want to make. You also have to be pretty sure you can tell a joke. But most important of all, you have to be certain that there is nothing offensive in your material. The truth is that when I started in this business, sales was pretty much an all-boys—and really all *white* boys—job. We could sit around and smoke big cigars and poke fun at everyone who wasn't us. But the world of business has become diversified. This diversity is a strength.

But it also means you need more sensitivity.

Lessons to learn from this chapter include these:

1. Humor can be an effective sales tool.
2. Everyone enjoys a good laugh, but different people have different funny bones. If you are using jokes as part of your presentation, you have to be certain that they cannot be misconstrued. Avoid controversial subjects. Avoid sexy subjects. You may want to avoid jokes altogether.
3. That doesn't mean you have to avoid humor. But humor should only be used within the context of your presentation. It should be used to help you make a point, not be the point.
4. In terms of PowerPoint, adding a cartoon to a badly thought-out slide does not make it better.

Chapter 20

Selling to Committees

The norm in selling is that you start out by making a cold-call. If things work out well, you get a meeting with a purchasing agent, a department manager, or (no matter what the title) the person at least partially responsible for buying what you sell. Then, if things work out well, after perhaps another meeting or two, you get to make a presentation in front of a larger group that ultimately will make the purchasing decision.

But it doesn't always work that way. The larger the sale, the more likely you are to be greeted by a committee on your *first* call, before you've had an opportunity to familiarize yourself with the company or any of its personnel. You're meeting strangers before you've had a chance to garner an ally. Everyone is coming into this cold.

The good news is that if several people do greet you at your first meeting, it means the company is serious about making a buy. In this day and age, when everyone is overworked, no company will commit the man-hours involved to meet with you (and presumably your competitors) if there isn't a strong interest in change.

This *probably* means that you already have overcome your biggest hurdle—the status quo—or at least are very close to achieving that goal. It doesn't mean that the company will place an order with *you*. But it does mean that the process will end with *someone* getting an order.

There's another positive. Chances are good that these are the people who will be making the final decision. In many ways this is better than dealing with an individual and then making a final presentation to a committee whose members you've never met before. That is almost like making another cold call.

In this situation, you have an opportunity to make the committee members into partners in your process from the very beginning. Just remember—you can also make them your adversaries.

There are numerous difficulties inherent in dealing with groups from the get-go. From your perspective, the purpose of any meeting—no matter how many people are involved—is to get an agreement to move on to the next step. Obviously this is easier when dealing with one person than with several (unless of course that person has multiple personalities, but that's another story).

In many ways, preparing to meet with a group on your *first* sales call is a lot easier than preparing to present to a group later in the process. Later in the process, you are expected to have done a lot more homework. Later in the process, you should have identified the players and the various axes they have to grind. Later in the process, you will probably have less opportunity to use a meeting as a way to gather information.

But since this is a first meeting and less is expected of you, invariably the folks attending are a lot more relaxed. This provides you with a greater opportunity to talk as opposed to sell.

Don't let me leave you with the wrong impression. It's important that you at least try to dig for info before any meeting. I always attempt due diligence before a first meeting with a committee. I always ask my contact, the person putting the meeting together, who the various players are and what their roles will be. And while I often get some answers, the replies are usually sketchy and incomplete. My contact usually does not know me—remember, this is before a first meeting—and therefore may not trust me enough to talk about his colleagues out of school.

The difference in this situation is that getting the information before a meeting is not as critical as it is later in the process. Again, in a first meeting with a committee you can be more open about needing information. Typically, I say something like this:

"Can you help me understand the role of everyone in the room?"

At this point, it's rare that I don't get the information I need—or at least the surface information I need. I still have to be watchful for clues that indicate who are the key people in the room and who are the gratuitous people there only for political reasons.

Ironically, that last person or group of people, the "gratuitous" ones, can be just as important to your sale as the people who have the final say-so. That gratuitous person usually knows he doesn't really belong at the meeting, and he often feels compelled to make, yes, gratuitous comments. And frankly, it's always easier to say something negative than positive.

So while she can't veto a sale, this person may be able to sink your chances by sowing discord and doubt. By doing so, she may make other committee members feel that they'd be better off in the status quo or with another supplier.

If your goal is to get consensus, to get group-think, it won't take much to upset the delicate balance you're looking for. So given the circumstances, it's really important that you get to know the people as intimately as you can in order to try to understand their individual agendas and see who is on your side.

Do not dismiss anyone. It's easy to focus on the person with the big title and ignore or pay only limited attention to the others.

In many ways, the immediate-group kind of arrangement is better for the salesperson because you get a feel pretty early on in terms of how you're doing. If you are not getting positive vibes after a couple of meetings with the committee, it's a sure sign that something is wrong.

There are several lessons to take away from this chapter:

1. It's important to get to know the people as quickly and intimately as possible.
2. Just as important, try to figure out their individual agendas.
3. Sort out the people who are on your team—and those who aren't.
4. Do not attempt to divide and conquer. It doesn't work. Committee members will be more loyal to their colleagues— even those they don't like—than they will ever be to you.
5. Never miscalculate by focusing on only one or two individuals.

Chapter 21

Closing and Follow-Up

You've given your presentation, and in an ideal situation, the stars are aligned. Everyone agrees that what you sell is not only perfect for the company, but you can deliver it where and when it's needed in just the right form that it's needed. Moreover, the price you charge not only allows you a nice profit, it is much cheaper than the company can get similar (and inferior) products anywhere else.

And then you wake up.

Surely, some dreams come true. But more often than not, the end of the presentation does not coincide with the end of your work on the account. I typically end my presentations by summarizing the main points I've already made:

- We'd like to work with you.
- Here's why we'd like to work with you.
- Here's why we think we are the right company for you.
- We share your vision. We understand what you are trying to accomplish.

If this is one of those dream-come-true moments (see above), you'll close the deal right then and there. Or someone will tell you, "Give me a call Tuesday and we'll finish this off."

However, usually the onus stays with you. You will have to follow up. Most salespeople say, "I'll call you in a week to get your reaction."

I don't believe in that. Unless I'm specifically told otherwise ("I'm going to be out of town. Check back with me in two weeks."), I always call back two to three days after a presentation so that it is still fresh in their minds. And I never start that conversation by saying "Do you have any questions?" or "Have you any thoughts about us?"

Your prospect is never prepared for your call or ready to ask you questions.

Instead, you should start the conversation by saying something like this: "I'd like to put together a work order" or "I'd like to block out dates for my seminars with you."

No matter what you sell, it's important that you know the company's ordering cycle. Does it place orders weekly, quarterly, or annually? Are supplies replenished on a continuing basis under terms of a contract that runs out next week, next month, next year? If you sell corporate insurance, are the company's existing policies coming up for renewal?

Knowing this cycle offers several advantages. First of all, it shows you are on top of the situation, that you've put some thought into the process, and that you know what's important. It makes you look good.

Second, when you do make the follow-up call, it's an easy way to get a meaningful conversation going: "I know the policy, contract, current buy cycle (pick one) is about up, so it might be a good time to start thinking about how to word a purchase order."

Finally, knowing the purchase cycle will let you know when it's time to start beating a dead horse. At a meeting in January, a potential client assured me he wanted me to address his national sales meeting in May. When I hadn't heard anything further from him by the beginning of March, I placed a call to him. A couple of weeks later, I placed another.

You'd think that a guy who is in charge of sales would have a little sympathy for a fellow salesperson and at the very least return a call. He didn't, but that happens, too. We've all met the guy (and excuse me, my experience is that it always is a guy) who is so wrapped up in himself he never returns calls.

Based on my couple of meetings with him, I didn't peg him to be like that. So I placed a couple of more calls, none of which was returned. Perhaps he was busy. Perhaps he really wanted to use me and was tied up. Perhaps I was delusional.

I knew that arrangements for his meeting would have to be finalized at least six to eight weeks in advance. When I didn't hear from him by early April, I knew it just wasn't going to happen. I'd missed that buy cycle, and I had to move on. Sometimes you just have to punt.

Most important, knowing the buy cycle is a good way to remind yourself that sometimes it ain't over, even though the fat lady sang.

A woman I know in Atlanta—let's say she sells widgets—gave what she thought was a brilliant presentation. When she left the conference room, she was certain she'd clinched a sale. But she was wrong. Somehow she'd misread one of the company's needs as well as the level of dissatisfaction with its existing widget supplier. Now let us move forward ten months. It is time for the company to reorder widgets. This woman refused to believe it was all over. She claimed she never heard the fat lady sing.

She wanted to go back in and make another presentation, a better presentation, but didn't know how to do it. The question is, how do you start another conversation when much of what you plan to say is exactly the same as the last conversation you had?

The salesperson came to me and described the situation. I advised her to admit that she made a mistake, to go back to her contact and be frank about it: "We missed the boat and we'd like another shot."

The salesperson was shocked. "I've been taught that you never apologize, never admit defeat, never say you did anything wrong."

When I asked her why, she was stumped. So she tried my idea, and her contact told her not to worry. Her original presentation wasn't off by as much as she thought, and she'd made some very good points. Moreover, the prospect told her where her first presentation had gone astray—all items easily correctible. Of course she could come back. And she did.

Because she knew the sales cycle, she knew when to hit the prospect again.

There are several lessons to take away from this chapter:

1. Don't wait a week or longer to follow up on a presentation. Call your contacts within a few days, when the presentation is still fresh in their minds.
2. Don't ask if they have any questions; ask for the sale.
3. Knowing the sell cycle for your product or service is helpful in many ways—most notably in terms of when the timing is best to ask for a contract.
4. Sometimes, if a prospect says one thing and does another, you may have to punt. Time is one of your assets. You don't want to waste it where someone clearly isn't interested.

5. If you made a mistake, don't be afraid to admit it. It's one way to restart a conversation and ignore any singing you may have heard in the background.

6. Sometimes it ain't over even when the fat lady has exited stage left to tumultuous applause.

Part Four

What Works for Presentations— And What Doesn't

Chapter 22

Case Study #1: Getting Everybody on the Same Page

Up until now, we've discussed the various elements of the sales process individually. What I intend to do now and in the next several chapters is give you brief case studies that take you through the entire progression from start to finish to see how smoothly it works—and how sometimes it doesn't.

In this chapter, I'm going to describe how my company, just a tiny drop in the ocean of globalization, was able to land a whale.

Getting Started

A number of years ago, I cold-called a small division of a large company. The person I spoke to, the sales manager, was receptive to a meeting, but was very up front about telling me that there really wasn't any project suitable for us at the time.

I replied, "Other people have told me the same thing. Why don't we get together to talk?"

Certainly that was no problem for me. The sales manager was located in New Jersey, less than an hour from my Manhattan office. Given the tremendous potential available if I landed this account, it was certainly worth the trip. While I had my eyes on an ambitious end game—that is, to eventually land business with the far larger parent company—even signing up this smaller division could be a profitable feather in our caps.

I didn't waste time asking for specifics of what the sales manager did or where his pain was. I'm a consultant, not a paramedic. The key to getting the conversation going was trying to accomplish something for the company.

The sales manager told me what he'd done when he came on board a few months earlier. He'd hired experienced salespeople and figured they would be able to do the job without vigorous sales training. This was the status quo I was fighting. I'm sure many people in my position would have given up. If you're selling sales training, and your prospect has purposely hired people he feels don't need sales training, why not punt?

Earlier in my career I might have. But I've heard about the fat lady and frankly I didn't hear her singing. Over the years, I developed the philosophy that as long as I can keep a conversation going, she's going to keep her mouth shut.

Moving Forward

We talked about how the manager's salespeople were doing, got into some of the numbers, and then we started talking more specifically about his goals. About ninety minutes into the conversation, I said this:

"It strikes me that there are a couple of ways we can work together, but I'm not sure yet."

He didn't understand why I wasn't sure yet and I told him that I had to put my thinking cap on. I said I didn't do generic one-size-fits-all presentations, and I wanted to factor in what he'd told me so that what we discussed would make sense to him.

In order to better understand how his company worked, I asked him for the names of several people I could talk to. The better my perspective, I told him, the better whatever proposal I came up with would be.

He gave me access to the company's chief financial officer and a couple of his managers—all of whom in turn led me to additional people. Although I'm not exactly certain now, I probably spoke to a dozen people, literally completing the Power of Twelve.

This did two things. Obviously I gathered important info, so I was able to speak from a perspective of wisdom when I made the presentation. But just as important, I probably gained some allies in doing the Power of Twelve. As I discussed my philosophy with them, I think they came to understand that I knew what I was doing.

They saw that I could help them and the company increase sales and earnings.

The CFO was actually the most helpful; others were less so. Almost invariably, some people were put off by my questions. They no doubt felt powerless, believing I was evaluating them and their work to report back to the boss. They did not accept my assurances to the contrary and remained wary. But that had no impact on me. In fact, it may have worked to my benefit because everyone knew something was going on. There wasn't going to be any shock if my proposals were accepted. And they could all claim that they had participated in the process.

I went back and discussed everything I'd learned with my team. Even though the company was staffed by experienced sales personnel and things were going relatively smoothly, there was definitely room for improvement. We concluded that we could go in and offer a full-scale sales school, nuts to bolts, but after much deliberation we decided that this might be too much for the prospect to absorb.

Outline Your Options

Remember, I had no reason to believe that the prospect was going to buy anything. So ten days after my initial meeting, I went back for a demonstration. By demonstration, of course, I don't mean taking out the product and showing him how to punch holes in paper. Rather, I gave him an idea of how he and his company could profit from the courses I proposed.

I brought three pieces of paper with me that outlined various possibilities and a fourth that was an overall summary of everything I proposed. Before I could say anything, he walked around from behind his desk, and we moved to a conference table so he could sit next to me and we could go over the sheets together. At that moment I realized that I had his interest and that he was the kind of guy I liked to work with—knowledgeable, open to new ideas, and not so caught up with himself that he would make this a kind of master-slave relationship.

We spoke about the sales school, which included three elements: appointment making, prospect management, and sales skills. I said I wasn't sure he needed the whole shebang because he'd hired experienced people. But the whole project made sense to him because it involved one systematic approach.

It wasn't that he or his salespeople were doing anything wrong. It's more that he became enticed by a concept he hadn't thought of. He was relatively new in the job. He had hired the salespeople, and he realized during our conversation that without a single consistent sales approach, it would be difficult for him to manage a staff of so many salespeople.

Additionally, I offered him the luxury of speed. He didn't have a year or so to see if his original arrangement would pan out. Using the training I proposed, everyone would be on the same page immediately.

I had my pen in hand, and as I went through the items on my list, I could make adjustments based on his reaction. In the end I walked away with fifteen different items from my original list of thirty that he felt made sense for him.

So we set another appointment in a few days' time. I'd verified my information, and I needed that much time to prepare a good presentation because this was one I really wanted to close on. We'd already talked about money. As I looked at the final piece, I was very comfortable, given that this essentially was a proposal the prospect had written with me.

I think it was Robert Burns who said: "The best laid schemes o' mice an' men / Gang aft a-gley."

(All right. I'm showing off a little. I just Googled that. But the point is life is like a good reliever—it throws curves at you.)

Think Fast

When I got there, the prospect asked if he could bring in two sales managers. What was I going to say, no? I wasn't angry at the idea; I was angry at me. What he did surprised me, and it shouldn't have. I was blindsided simply because I didn't think to ask who else would be at the presentation.

But, despite my years, I am like a ballet dancer—that is how quick on my feet I am. I adjusted because that was the only option available to me. It took me a few minutes to put two and two together, but I'd spoken to both the sales managers on the phone as part of my Power of Twelve. They were helpful in answering my questions but not overly enthusiastic. My impression was that they didn't know what to make of me.

So I stepped up to the barre and went to work. I asked them if they were familiar with what had been discussed in the first meeting. They gave me a sort of unconvincing mumbled yes. The good news was that since I'd at least spoken to them, they were part of the team that helped create the presentation. It meant that they didn't have to criticize the proposal the way people almost automatically do when asked what they think.

The bad news was that to be sure everyone was on the same page, I had to go back to explain how I had reached the present stage. I went over the high points, but that unnecessarily made the presentation longer than it should have been.

Then I went on to the PowerPoint demonstration. I needed only a few slides to make my message clear. (Some are included, with commentary, at the end of this chapter.) However, my main point was *not* the program I wanted to do for them but the benefits it would provide them. The product doesn't matter; the only thing that matters is what it can accomplish for the customer.

In the end I got the business, but it really wasn't the end. It was only the beginning. Now the issue was how I could penetrate the other and much larger divisions of this company.

Sales Is About Relationships...Sometimes

I've said in the past that sales is about product, not relationships. Also, the salesperson's worst enemy is the status quo. Now might be a good time to modify that stand slightly. When *you* have an account, the status quo is your friend. And relationships do matter at this point—especially if you're delivering what you promised when you first landed the business. People change jobs, and they remember those folks who made their previous work easier and stress-free.

My contact was eventually promoted to head of sales of a much larger division in the multinational company. Over the year or so that we worked together, I'd been tempted to network through him to see if he'd recommend me to his counterparts in other divisions. I'd sort of hinted, but he didn't volunteer and I didn't press him. For one thing, in a company of that size—it had about 60,000 employees around the world—not everyone knows everyone else. My man might have known the name of the guy I had to see in Division X, but he might not have known him, and therefore he might have been reluctant to recommend me—even though we had a great relationship and my courses had really helped him, as I said they would.

I stayed in touch with him after I finished my assignment. When I found out about his big promotion, I immediately thought that could be a shot for me to take the good work I'd done and move up the corporate ladder. The question was, how could I up-sell this? How could I get him to see me as a global player?

I gave him a little time to settle in and then got in touch to arrange an appointment. I brought two of my best trainers with me to give him a sense of security. I didn't want him to think that he was dealing with a one-person shop. The first thing I did when we met was to tell him about some of the new things we'd been doing, some of the bigger projects we'd handled since I last worked for him. He was intrigued, but hiring us again wasn't simple. Is it ever?

The company, hoping to reorganize, had contracted with a major consulting firm. It was paying the consultants big bucks, and it just didn't make sense for him to go off on his own without at least checking with them.

The consulting company, of course, had its own agenda and it didn't involve me. They felt they were capable of doing everything, including sales training. To overcome their objections, I knew I'd need to make a full-scale presentation. With the help of my original contact, I was able to use the Power of Twelve. He gave me permission to talk to the consultants, and I met with every person on their team. I flew overseas to the division's corporate headquarters where my contact had set up appointments.

I met with the division CEO (my contact's boss) and told him what I was trying to do. I worked my way down to sales managers and even a few sales reps. As I got deeper into the company, I got a much clearer picture of what they wanted to accomplish. Also, as I communicated what I wanted to and could do, I felt I picked up some allies along the way.

But that didn't really resolve my problem. The major obstacle remained the consulting company, which I thought was trying to sabotage any deal. I had to prove to them that I had the global capability to handle a program as large as this one. So I set up a group presentation with the head of the consulting unit, my prospect, a financial guy for the division, and two of the division's country heads. The meeting was held in Europe. I brought three people with me: a German trainer, a British trainer, and a writer.

I gave a PowerPoint presentation that my staff and I had developed over three weeks that described the following:

1. Our global capability
2. Our corporate structure
3. My understanding of the company (without pointing out where they were having problems; concentrating instead on being positive about its goals)
4. What the total package would look like

This last point included a description of what our role would be, as well as the responsibilities of the consulting company and the customer. We emphasized that the consulting company would take the lead except in sales training. We'd take a secondary role and the company would be the overall arbiter.

The people asked a lot of questions—most of which we were prepared for. We answered in German and English. However, there was an issue we didn't anticipate. The consultant wondered how we could guarantee that the training would be the same all over the world, since many of our European trainers were not staffers but freelancers. The quality control issue was one, frankly, I wasn't prepared for. But the German trainer picked up the ball. Speaking accented English, he described how long he'd been with us, how many programs he did, and how well he knew the subject matter.

Next Steps

We decided that the next step would be for me to meet with my contact again to get a reaction to this meeting. It turned out that we had convinced him that we had the capability to do the training, but he wasn't sure the consulting company agreed.

The issue now was how much more money I wanted to invest in what appeared to be a losing battle with the consulting company. That turned out to be a simple decision. We'd reached the tipping point; I couldn't back out.

The consulting company was going to hold a meeting (yes, in Europe) with all the players to flesh out the entire picture. I asked my contact to include me in this meeting and he agreed he would bring me into it. He did, and I spent two days in this meeting—but as a peer, not a supplicant. I gave my opinion when applicable, and at no time did I allow anyone to minimize my company's expertise. I also used the opportunity to build some rapport with the meeting participants. I'd shipped copies of some of my books ahead of me and gave them out.

I don't know if the books turned the trick or whether it was my winning personality, but I was asked to make another presentation right then and there. I was prepared. I whipped out essentially the same proposal I'd done before, though it was a little more specific about what I'd do. It also used some of the buzz words the consulting company was apparently fond of.

We had another meeting, and I eventually landed a deal that was worth about a million bucks.

Important Takeaways

There are several lessons here:

1. Good relationships don't make a sale, but they can get you in the door. I always stay in touch with every happy client, even if she moves to a job that doesn't carry training responsibilities. You never know where that client will go next.
2. Out of little acorns, mighty oaks grow. The acorn was that first assignment with the small division. The mighty oak was the larger division. It's a reason I don't allow myself any off

days. As an entrepreneur (and all salespeople are entrepreneurs), I feel that every presentation holds the key to all my future business.

3. You have to climb every mountain. As I look back on it, I find it amazing that I had the chutzpah to try to land as big a client as this. But I had confidence in myself and in what I was selling. My training worked.

4. Sometimes you have to invest money to make money. The back-and-forth travel to Europe cost me a fortune. But I still have this client, so it was a small investment considering the return.

Reviewing the Presentation

As I look back at my presentation, only four words come to mind: *"What was I thinking?!"*

I can't figure it out. Well, I can figure it out—I'm just ashamed to admit it. I had a slide of a globe. I suppose I wanted somehow to illustrate my worldwide capabilities. But all I did was show a globe with the words "The World" written on top of it (Slide 1). In retrospect, I'd have been better off with a map that showed where the prospect's learning centers were and how they coordinated with my field offices.

Slide 1

Then I gave them a slide of our corporate structure (Slide 2). I'm not sure of why this prospect needed to know our corporate structure; I think I would have been better off if I . . . heck, I'd have been better off if I just left this slide off.

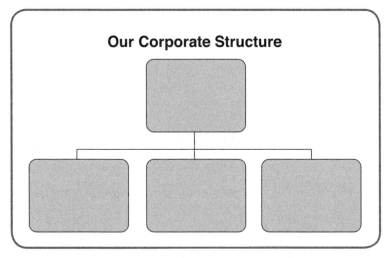

Slide 2

Finally, we get to the slide that most amazes me. I did a diagram of their corporate structure (Slide 3). Of all the useless slides I've ever done over the course of my career, this has to rank right up there.

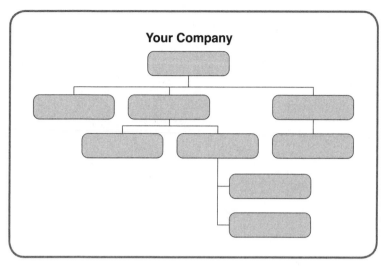

Slide 3

There are several important lessons here:

1. Do as I say, not as I do.
2. Even the smartest professionals screw up presentations. But if you are still able to convey that you have the right product for the right price, you can still salvage a deal.

Chapter 23

Case Study #2: Expensive Lessons

I read a lot of biographies and autobiographies about people of accomplishment. If there is one thread they have in common, it's that they all claim to learn more from their mistakes than their successes. I offer the following chapter based on the assumption that what they have written is true. And it must be. Because I made a significant mistake that I expect will never, ever happen again.

The Beginning

The prospect was an international data storage company. Every year the company holds a large international sales meeting attended by about 1,000 people. There are breakout sessions and tours of the area where the meeting is held and, each year, there is a motivational speaker. It's usually someone like a mountain climber or a person who has overcome a tremendous obstacle to become successful.

Several years ago, I received a call from the firm asking if I'd be interested in being that year's motivational speaker. Though I am not an athlete and I haven't overcome a major obstacle, I do give motivational speeches. It's not something I do a lot of, but I still do them regularly—perhaps a half-dozen times a year.

This is not a big part of my business and (though I don't remember for certain) I may have been busy preparing a *really important* presentation. Whatever the reason, I didn't take the time to prepare anything special.

I met with three members of the team planning this event and gave them my canned speech presentation. The speech runs sixty to ninety minutes; it's called Guidelines for Success or (if they'd like) Guidelines for Success and Failure, and blah, blah, blah. I have a PowerPoint presentation, but I frequently (including this time) ignore it. I gave it my best shot, but I realized I was Mr. Bland. It wasn't something I really worried about. If I got it, fine. If not, that was okay too.

I wasn't expecting too much because I realized that to the three people I met with, I was just a generic speaker. As far as they were concerned, there were a million guys like me.

Given that I'm writing about this meeting, it's a safe bet that I got the assignment. About three months later, I delivered my speech to rave reviews. Afterwards, in fact, the head of the division—the boss of the three men who interviewed me initially—came over and said to me:

"There's a lot of opportunity here for you and I'd like to pursue this with you." He appeared to be extremely receptive to my message. In that brief conversation, I learned something important. I promised myself I would never again be blasé when asked to make a speech because there is no way to know where that will lead. Henceforth, my presentations about my speech would be as detailed, as well planned, and as well executed as every one of my sales presentations.

The First Presentation

I called him and didn't get a response. I called him a second time and still got no call back. Finally, on my third try, I got him, and we agreed to a meeting in Philadelphia in about two weeks' time. I followed my standard procedure. I had made some assumptions about the company based on my experience at the sales meeting. They were wrong, but the division head corrected me, so now I had a pretty good handle on the company and its sales force.

I came back a couple of weeks later with a preliminary outline to be sure I was on target and asked to come back with a full-blown presentation. I did and it was one of those presentations salespeople dream about. I explained what I wanted to do, a three-day sales session with appropriate follow-up. I went into detail not only about the program but its benefits to the company's sales organization. I had a fifteen-page handout and an executive summary that was easy to skim, logical, and apparently very persuasive.

If I told you they loved it that would be an understatement. They were ecstatic and couldn't wait for me to start. I did ten of these programs around the country and subsequently did another in Europe.

CASE STUDY #2: EXPENSIVE LESSONS

The Second Presentation

About eighteen months later, out of the blue, I got a call from the company's number-two guy in Europe. He said he was very impressed with what we'd done. The company was thinking about rolling out the program in all of Europe and Asia, and he was convinced without a doubt that we could help.

So we flew to Madrid. I brought four people with me, English-, Spanish- and French-speaking trainers as well as a writer who helped prepare the presentation. What I didn't bring was my memory. It wasn't that long ago that I had vowed never to come unprepared to another meeting. At the time, I was specifically referring to a meeting about a speech. Still, I should have been smarter.

There were a couple of things I didn't know going into the presentation. I didn't know that we were competing against three other companies—only two of which were mentioned and then only peripherally. Also, and this was my big mistake, I didn't know as much about the company as I thought I did.

Based on my conversation with the number-two guy and my previous experience with the company, I assumed this contract was in the bag. Moreover, I thought the presentation was just a formality—and I treated it that way. I didn't do any preparation and gave the same presentation that I'd created for the U.S. division several years earlier.

There were two people there, my contact and his boss, the head of European operations. The Big Boss listened to my presentation and clearly was not a fool. He got up and said, "This is a very generic presentation. Something you could have given to anybody."

He was right. It was absolutely indefensible. Everyone was embarrassed, especially the number-two guy, who'd brought us in. The writer who accompanied us tried to save the day. He did a flip-chart presentation that seemed to interest the boss. He ordered lunch in and appeared to be engrossed in what was going on. The writer was drawing diagrams, and it looked as though this was working.

We left the meeting believing we'd done an adequate though far from good job convincing the Big Boss that we were a good company. We also felt we had a shot at this. When we asked, we were told that in very vague terms that we were competing against two other firms.

About five days later, we were told that another training company, one that had never been mentioned, won the contract.

The Third Presentation

About six months later I got a call from number two again, and yes, the company was moving in a new direction, and I absolutely, positively had a good chance this time around. I flew to Madrid again, and we had an informal discussion. He provided me with a great deal more insight that I'd had previously. Almost immediately I could visualize what the presentation should include and how I'd design it. We set a time for a formal presentation, but three weeks before that date (still well after I'd invested considerable extra funds), the presentation was cancelled. Number one was moving the company in a new direction.

Important Takeaways

There are several lessons here, which unfortunately are ones I had to pay for to learn myself:

1. I consider myself a professional. For goodness sakes, I *teach* sales. I write books about sales. The only way I can console myself is with the knowledge that even the best pros are not perfect. NBA players don't hit every shot from the free throw line where no one guards them. The last man to get four hits every ten times he came to the plate was Ted Williams. But this was the equivalent of stepping up to the plate or foul line and swinging or shooting with your eyes closed. There are righteous sales and losses. By righteous, I mean you go in and do your very best. Win, lose or draw, you know you gave it your all. What we did here was sloppy; we didn't deserve the sale. Hopefully we learned from this mistake.
2. Most important, I twice took presentations for granted, first when I was asked to give the speech and later when I flew to Madrid the first time. It's important not to forget the basics and go through them step by step. It will make you a bet-

ter salesperson. I considered the motivational speeches more pain-in-the-neck than opportunity, and I presented in a kind of cavalier way that reflected my lack of interest. Traveling to meetings to give these speeches was time consuming (this one was in Chile) and took me away from work that paid far more. But of course I missed the boat. Usually I gave those speeches at meetings of existing clients. It didn't occur to me (though it certainly should have) how great an opportunity this was to prospect for new business. That will not happen again.

In terms of the second presentation, we assumed because of our success in the United States (and the one European program) we would get the business in Europe and that whatever cultural issues came up could be smoothed over. (There's no need to repeat what happens when you assume. It's just annoying when it happens to you.) I got lucky once when I got the speaking job, which led to a U.S. assignment. I got what I deserved in Madrid.

3. Not only did I take the contract for granted, but I just skipped over basic steps in the process. Instead of concentrating on the next step, my thoughts were only on the contract. I based my entire thinking process on what number two told me— essentially, that I had the contract. So I didn't bother with the Power of Twelve. I knew nothing about the top man, what he was thinking, or the company's real-time power structure. I assumed (again) that number two had some authority. When the contract went to a company I wasn't even aware was in the competition, I began to think that the entire process was orchestrated before it began. There exists the possibility in the back of my mind that even the best presentation wouldn't have gotten me the business. Of course, in the back of my mind is the recognition that that might just be sour grapes.

4. This presentation cost me a small fortune in airline tickets alone. I understand this is just the cost of doing business. But it reminded me of another important lesson: Never underestimate the importance of frequent flier miles.

Reviewing the Presentation

The presentation materials in this example were better than in the previous case study, but were still far from perfect.

Look at Slide 1, which says "Why Training Works" and tell me why training works. Because it helps you make better graphs? Or pie charts? Or cute pictures of little girls?

I actually forget now, but I assume I was trying to make a point. It would have been far better to put each illustration in a separate slide and add brief text offering at least a hint of what the illustrations mean.

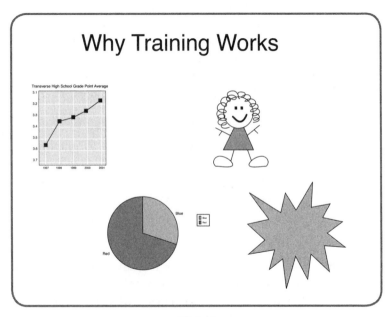

Slide 1

Similarly, don't put twenty points on one slide, like I did on Slide 2. (To avoid sharing this company's information, I put X's where I had individual programs in the original presentation.) It's just too much.

The Training Program

1. XXX
2. XXX
3. XXX
4. XXX
5. XXX
6. XXX
7. XXX
8. XXX
9. XXX
10. XXX

11. XXX
12. XXX
13. XXX
14. XXX
15. XXX
16. XXX
17. XXX
18. XXX
19. XXX
20. XXX

Slide 2

Chapter 24

Case Study #3: Don't Copy What These Salespeople Do

Everything I've written up to now is based on my years of experience. But as I'm sure you know, people see things through the lens of their own experience. Four, five, or six pairs of eyes can witness the same incident but interpret it differently. In this chapter, therefore, I intend to provide a different perspective, that of a purchasing agent for an extremely large *Fortune* 500 company.

The Setup

I happened to be in his office for part of what I'm about to describe, but he filled me in. So, though he will not collect a penny of the royalties on this book (one of many reasons I'm keeping his identity secret), what follows essentially is me channeling my friend.

While apparently conducting some other business, a copier company salesman had been up to this corporate office. On this visit, he noticed that the copying machines in use were not up to the quality of his product. He called up the purchasing agent and said he couldn't figure out why he wasn't doing business with the company and that he'd like to set up an appointment to discuss it.

"I thought it was a pretty good approach. I know there are differences in copiers—some print faster, print colors better, use cheaper paper," my friend said. "But for the most part I consider them a generic product. Besides, the copiers we were using were more than adequate for our current needs. But I decided to see him, anyway. I thought his approach was a little different. Usually salespeople start off talking about their products. That's the last thing I want to discuss on a first phone call."

Lack of Professionalism

But once the salesperson got into the purchasing agent's office, there was no more novelty. "First of all, he came in carrying his jacket," the purchasing agent said. "It was a very warm day, but he came early and was out in the reception area for several minutes before I brought him in. That was more than enough time for him to cool down and put his jacket back on. I know you may call me old-fashioned, but you're in a business setting and you should dress appropriately. We weren't at a Knicks game."

Bringing Guests

The salesman then compounded his felony by bringing his manager along. That was kind of understandable from his point of view. He felt the company held unlimited sales potential. In discussions back in his office, the salesman did some quick math and figured the prospect could be good for as many as 500 copiers. That would be the biggest sale he ever made—and in fact the single biggest sale in the history of his company. Bringing his sales manager with him may have made sense from his point of view, but just as a courtesy (if nothing else) he should have mentioned it to the prospect.

"In the big scheme of things it probably isn't that big a deal, but when I came out to the reception area to bring him in, I was caught a little off guard when the salesguy introduced his boss. You might think I'm a control freak—and maybe I am—but I don't like surprises. I thought bringing his manager was a little rude. I felt almost as though they were going to gang up on me.

"The truth is that if he'd told me in advance, I would have told him not to [bring the manager]. There wasn't—at least at that point— a level of interest on my part that would warrant this kind of overkill. Something might have developed, but I was in a negative frame of mind before he came into my office—and of course his 'presentation' didn't make things better."

Poor Presentation

Unbeknownst to the purchasing agent, the salesman had a leg up. He knew his copiers (as I later found out) were far superior to what the company was using, but he didn't take advantage and use that information to trigger a discussion. Instead, he immediately took out his laptop and started a PowerPoint presentation.

"To start with, I had a bad view of the screen. Plus the sound on the laptop was terrible. Then, he goes over in full detail every one of the seventeen slides. How do I know there were seventeen? Because I counted, that's how I know. One by one by one. The slides talked about his company, talked about price points and customer service. They never mentioned me, my company, or what our needs were and how they could fulfill them. It was a generic presentation, and it was one that he probably gives at every sales call, regardless of the company."

There was nothing in the presentation that grabbed the potential buyer. "I was disappointed because our initial conversation on the phone was different from what I normally get. I expected something from the salesman. But what he gave me was very pedestrian. Worse than pedestrian. It was awful. Maybe my expectations were too high."

After concluding his presentation, the salesman committed what is probably the most common and egregious error in the business. Instead of moving on to the next step or trying to get either additional information or verifying what little he knew, the salesman asked if the prospect had any questions.

"What questions could I have? I was turned off early, clearly (I thought) uncomfortable and not paying attention. When I said I really had none and started to get from my seat the sales manager spoke for the first time. He said, 'You must have some questions.'

"What became pretty clear to me is that the two of them hadn't even bothered to coordinate the presentation. I know some people rehearse, but since this was a boilerplate presentation, I doubt a rehearsal was necessary. But I don't think they even spoke about it. I have no idea why the sales manager came. He didn't contribute anything to the conversation and kind of stood mutely by while his sales rep was floundering.

"Honest to goodness, if one of my salespeople did so badly, I'd be embarrassed."

Salvaging a Deal

Trying to salvage the situation, the rep said "I think I have an idea. Why don't you let me put in one of our units in your office for a week and let's try it out? This is a first-class machine. You don't have to worry about staples screwing it up. And I'm sure you see long lines of admin assistants and even executives at your current copier. This machine is so fast that it will eliminate those lines."

My friend's response: "I must have really had a puzzled look on my face because I never stood on line. I never heard about lines at the copy machine and was unaware that this was a problem. But this guy was not going to be stopped. He upped the offer to a free machine for a month at no cost. But cost wasn't the issue. It served no purpose to replace the existing units; they were leased and there were significant early-termination penalties.

"I know a lot of people in my kind of position who have a closed door policy. They won't see anyone unless they've identified a particular need. If it works for them, fine. I see people to the extent that I can because you never know what's out there. But this particular sales rep made me question my policy. It was almost a complete waste of time."

Subsequently, the sales rep went back to his computer, did some calculations over the course of several long and silent moments and came up with a comparison of what he guessed the prospect was paying on his current lease and what it would cost if he installed his machines.

The first thing the sales rep did wrong was to guess what the lease costs were. He didn't even bother to ask the purchasing agent. "I don't know if I would have told him, but that's a moot point, because he didn't ask." So not surprisingly, the numbers he came up with were all wrong. He based his figures on a standard lease, not considering the fact that the company he was selling to is so large it could work out far more favorable terms with its suppliers.

Secondly, he didn't ask about the costs of terminating current copier agreements early and didn't factor that in.

"He told me his copiers would save me $16 a month each," the purchasing agent told me. "When you're talking 500 machines throughout the corporation, that's a nice piece of change. I told him I'd look into it and get back to him if I was interested.

"I did look into it and his numbers were off by a factor of $16 a month a machine. When you took everything into consideration, his offer was almost exactly the same as what we were now getting.

"I keep a vendor file on big-ticket items—cars, computers and the like. And my original intention was to listen to this guy and if he made sense explain we were not currently in the market but that he definitely would hear from me when the lease was up. This guy was such a poor representative of his company, I doubt I'll make that call."

As a footnote to this fiasco, the PowerPoint presentation was intended to replace a brochure the company previously left behind on sales calls. "So there wasn't even a good reference piece for me to put into the file if I'd wanted to."

A Second Example

A good salesperson will find this story hard to believe. I didn't because almost the same thing happened to me. I also had a copier machine guy come into my office hoping to sell me a copier. He spoke to my administrative assistant to get some information on how we used our copier. She was nice to him. He was nice to her. And then he spent some time with me.

He had a generic flip-chart presentation that he went through very quickly. But he failed to ask what my plans were for the company. Was I looking to expand it? Were my copying needs going to grow?

Because I am a wonderful and sympathetic person, I told him that I was in the market for was a high-speed printer that I could use to print and bind my school material. My intention was to set that up as a separate profit center.

He told me he didn't handle high-speed printers, but that he would have someone else in the company call me. No one ever did. I don't know (and frankly I don't care) whether he forgot to pass my name along or he did pass my name on and someone at the end dropped the ball. But of course I couldn't check because he was in such a rush to leave he forgot to leave a business card.

The sales rep was not some young newcomer to the business. He was an experienced guy who told me he'd been at this for a long time and knew his products backwards and forwards. But he wasn't a warrior. There are something like 700 copiers sold every hour in the United States. If you wait long enough, that machine is going to break and need to be replaced. This rep was a waiter, an order taker.

Important Takeaways

There are several lessons here, assuming you want to avoid the examples of the two hapless copier salespeople above:

1. Do your homework. Among the biggest enemies you have is time. You're wasting it if you visit a prospect and immediately give a presentation without attempting to find out anything about how he currently does business. In the case of my friend the purchasing manager, the sales rep had made a good first impression, which he quickly ruined by immediately diving into a nonspecific presentation that had no impact on a potential customer. Sales is a process. You skip steps at your own peril.

2. Never assume you know everything. The sales rep in this case assumed that he could resolve the status quo issue by talking about a better machine. He didn't take into account the company's existing lease, the cost of terminating the lease, or what they were paying. So all his financial projections were inaccurate. The purchasing manager probably would have been cooperative in providing necessary information about the company's copier use. And while the rep still wouldn't have made an immediate sale, he could have made a better impression (and perhaps a sale down the road).

3. No one likes surprises, birthday and bachelor parties aside. You don't like to walk into a presentation attended by people you didn't expect or even in numbers you hadn't anticipated. The same works the other way. If you are going to bring someone to a meeting, let the other party know. It's just polite.

4. You only get one shot at making a good first impression. Your appearance counts, and you should dress and present yourself professionally.
5. Always leave behind something, even if it's only a business card.
6. Always follow up on your promises. The sales rep who came to my office should have checked to see that someone from the high-speed copier end of his business contacted me. As it turned out, we changed our plans and might have needed a new regular-speed copier for the office. But I'm wary when a sales rep doesn't provide good service while he's trying to woo me; what can I get after I'm locked into a contact?

Reviewing the Presentation

I was going to leave this blank and let you fill in what was wrong, but this turned out to be a lot of fun. Mostly because this wasn't one I wrote or approved.

Simply unless you are making a specific point, you don't need slides showing various copiers. And if you are making a point, you need to somehow explain it. For example, there could have been text explaining the capabilities of each copier or the monthly leasing costs. But pictures of copiers by themselves are probably best left in brochures.

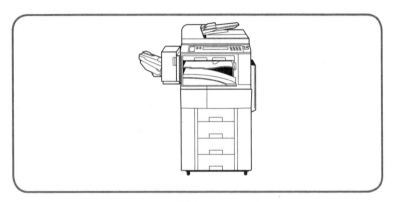

Slide 1

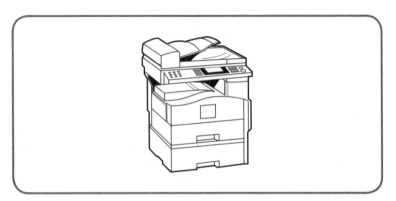

Slide 2

Slide 3

Chapter 25

Case Study #4: Know What Your Customer Needs

One of the most difficult things to do in the sales process is to make a presentation on a technical subject. The main reason for this *should* be obvious. Typically the audience is mixed, so technical specs need to be dumbed down to a marketing executive's level. At the same time, the content can't be so basic that you lose the attention of the tech people in the room. It's not easy.

Please note, however, that I said this *should* be obvious. But one of the most common mistakes salespeople make is that in preparing presentations of this nature, they go to one extreme or the other. These presentations are often filled with so much technical jargon that anyone who is not an engineer or scientist can't figure out what's being said. Or, at the other extreme, the presentation is so simplistic that it belies the technical advances the product may hold.

There are other dangers as well. I've seen presentations that were so technical even the technically oriented members of the audience were confused. Beyond that, in the process of attempting to provide all the technical data in a comprehensive—and comprehensible—way, salespeople lost sight of the marketing aspects of what they were trying to sell. It's not easy, as the following story makes clear.

Selling to a Technical Audience

I worked with a heating and air conditioning contractor located in Pittsburgh. This is a company that had no problem getting initial appointments because it had an innovative approach—but it lacked the ability to close the sale.

Typically, the company's salespeople called prospects about maintenance contracts. This is an extremely difficult sale. My experience is that most people don't think about maintenance until something goes wrong. This company sold contracts to larger commercial accounts—apartment and commercial buildings—but the principle was pretty much the same as for private houses. I know I don't have a maintenance contract with anyone for the heating and air conditioning units in my home.

In this case, not only does a salesman have to sell his product, he has to demonstrate a need for it. It's not like your prospect is already using a competitor's product—he doesn't even see the need for it. That's a tough sell. Tough? It's almost surreal.

Before the Presentation

But this heating and air conditioning company had an innovative—dare I say unique?—approach. What the company's sales reps would tell prospects was, "We can't make an intelligent presentation unless we know your situation." So they offered prospects a free top-to-bottom inspection of their heating and cooling systems. The only thing the rep asked in return was an opportunity to present his people's findings. Certainly the price was right, and most people agreed. It was hard not to.

This was a significant investment on the part of the heating company. They'd bring in a technician who'd start at the roof and work his way down to the basement. Typically, the checkup took three hours or more. After analyzing the results, the sales rep called to set up a time for a formal presentation.

The Presentation Itself

The company wanted to make it a major event and issued a blanket invitation, asking that all the people involved in this area come in. But the rep didn't ask for specifics, and he never knew who would be there or what the responsibilities were of the people who did attend. The sales rep was usually accompanied by a manager and the technician who had conducted the survey. They brought coffee, doughnuts, and a confusing PowerPoint.

The first slide was a history of the company, explaining what it did. The slide was barely legible.

Slide two was an explanation of how the company conducted the heating system survey. This slide was legible.

Slide three was a schematic of the company's heating system. The sales rep went through it step by step, explaining the complexities of various parts of the system, such as the chiller. This part of the presentation made the least sense. I knew nothing about heating systems, and the explanation the sales rep gave was far too technical for me. And I was not alone.

I spoke to some of the attendees at a couple of these presentations that I attended, and the reaction was always the same. People who were in the business end of the company didn't understand this part of the presentation, while the technical folks found the presentation too simplistic. "It was like giving an elementary school lesson to college students," one of them told me.

But it was with the fourth slide that the company really went astray. Here it explained how it would reconfigure the heating and air conditioning system. That was the company's hidden agenda. It wasn't really after a maintenance contract; it wanted to install a new multimillion-dollar system.

What was wrong with that? So much, really, that I don't know where to begin. First of all, the people attending the presentation were expecting a sales pitch on maintenance. So they were unprepared for one that involved an expenditure of this size. Also, it's very likely that the people who would approve a maintenance contract and the ones who'd okay a large capital expenditure like a new or newly modified heating system are different. So the sales rep was likely making the wrong presentation to the wrong people.

But even if they were the right people, this is not what they were there for. And this presentation smacks of something seedy, a kind of high-end bait-and-switch. Consequently, by the time the sales rep got to the fifth slide—about the efficiencies of the new system and how much money it might save the prospect—he'd already lost the audience.

I suggested that as part of its initial process, the heating and air conditioning company just go after the maintenance business, instead of immediately trying to switch to a new installation. It's more important to establish yourself as a reputable company first and then suggest the more profitable new or reconfigured heating system.

The company adopted my suggestion. I'm happy to say that its sales increased 19 percent in the first year and have increased by double digits every year since then.

A Second Example

Of course, not everyone takes my suggestions. We worked with a solar energy company in California that overall was doing extremely well. It had identified hospitals as potentially good customers and created a separate division to go after this market. But it wasn't working out as expected.

The Positives

The company had a lot going for it. First of all, it was based in sunny Southern California. Second, it had a product that actually reduced a customer's costs. Third, in some instances, it even enabled a company to *make* money by selling any excess electricity its solar panels generated back to the grid. And finally, the state offered substantial tax incentives to companies that installed solar panels.

Also, the company was very sharp in the way it made its presentations, taking advantage of the latest technology. For example, it was able to tell how much sunlight every community in the entire country might expect in a given year. And then it was able to extrapolate from that how much a company could save on its electricity bill. This worked well for a number of reasons. These were obviously valid sales points. But more important, I think, they reflected technological know-how from a company in a very high-tech field. If I were a potential customer, I'd certainly feel more confident in this firm's ability to harness the latest technology than another company that came in and drew flip-chart pictures.

The Negatives

But as we shall see, technology isn't the be-all and end-all. If your presentation doesn't make sense to the customer, it doesn't matter that it has every bell and whistle ever invented. You're not going to close the sale. And this company certainly had a powerful PowerPoint.

It started off quickly explaining how the production of solar energy could actually make the hospital money. In succeeding slides, it gave estimates for the hospital's current costs, estimated cost savings, and estimated earnings at current rates for the excess electricity the solar panels will generate. There was even a slide—and this was a nice touch—showing an architect's rendering of what the building would look like with solar panels installed.

There were some cute slides about the ease of maintenance. (The company felt that anyone who was environmentally conscious would also have a sense of humor. And it may be right. At each of the presentations I saw, the audience laughed at the appropriate times when slides flashed on the screen showing maintenance staff with nothing to do.)

What Went Wrong

Why then couldn't the company close the deals? The answer was in the last group of slides, which talked about the cost of the panels and installation. Even with tax incentives, it took thirty years for customers to recoup the cost of the investment. So the solar energy company had two problems.

First, such a large investment in construction required the approval of the hospital board of directors. But the solar energy company never delved deeply enough into the Power of Twelve to even try to get board members involved. The people who attended its presentation generally weren't empowered to even recommend purchases at that level, and even those with that power were reluctant to take the matter to the board.

Which brings us to the real problem. The solar energy company made a mistake in targeting hospitals. From a distance, trying to sell to hospitals *seemed* to make sense. After all, like the solar energy company, they are technologically advanced, utilizing the latest in MRIs and scans.

But there is a difference. The technology the hospital uses brings in business. You go to a hospital to get an MRI, not because the lighting is good. Also, while expensive, the payout is a lot faster than thirty years—as anyone who recently has paid a hospital bill knows. Frankly, the equipment doesn't *last* thirty years, so obviously the payout is a lot faster than that.

In hospitals the largest single expense is labor; energy accounts for less than 8 percent of costs. So there is no incentive for hospitals to sign up for high-initial-cost alternative energy source.

We told that to the company's sales manager, but he was apparently wedded to this concept he had introduced. I suspect it was a matter of pride on his part. Or maybe it was just office politics. But, in either case, when we saw he wouldn't be moved, we stepped back. We might have signed a sales training contract with this company, but if its executives were not prepared to change basic policy, we'd all wind up losers in the end.

There are several lessons in this chapter:

1. Don't bait and switch. It is counterproductive to come in and tell your prospect that you want to make a presentation about "A" and then try to sell a more expensive "B." Years ago, a car salesman tried to do that to me. Not only have I never gone back into that dealership again, but I never bought that brand of automobile again. People don't like to be played for fools.
2. Don't always shoot for the moon. You are better off getting a small piece of business and using that to parlay into something bigger and more profitable—especially if that small piece of business is something you're likely to sell.
3. Know your audience. Be sure it's the right one for your message. Don't give a highly technical presentation to lay people, and don't talk down to the technicians. It's a tough balancing act, especially if the audience is mixed, but it certainly improves your odds of making a sale.
4. You are making a sale that involves the latest technology. You want the presentation to be cool and reflect your technological ability. However, you cannot lose sight of the basics. If

the deal doesn't make sense, all the bells and whistles won't clinch a sale for you.

5. Time is your enemy, and it's silly to waste it by trying to go after prospects who are prospects only in your mind.

6. Finally, and I quote the great salesman Kenny Rogers, "You got to know when to hold 'em, know when to fold 'em; know when to walk away, know when to run." I have said repeatedly in this book that one of the biggest enemies salespeople have is time. It doesn't make any sense to waste it pursuing unlikely clients. It makes less sense to let pride (or politics) interfere with your judgment.

Conclusion

Yes, there is some logic to my madness. I ended one of the last chapters with the story of a saleswoman who refused to take "no" for an answer. She refused to listen when others claimed they heard the fat lady sing.

It wasn't so much that she'd been screwed over (as I had) by a customer; she'd screwed up, knew it and had the unmitigated chutzpah to refuse to give up. She was determined to fight another round.

At the beginning of this book, I spoke a little about the difference between salespeople and order takers. My suspicion is that if you've gotten this far, you are a salesperson. And if I'm right, you know that there are no magic pills. There is no potion you can take that will help you clinch a sale.

There is a certain purity in the sales process. You get out of it what you put in of yourself. A fancy presentation is meaningless if your vision and the customer's vision aren't aligned. Ultimately, success or failure rests with you, and your understanding of the customer's needs, your drive, and your willingness to persevere even when many people feel the aria is over.

The lessons you learned here can and will help you. But please do not for one minute think that they can substitute for your contributions.

Good luck.

INDEX

Practical and proven strategies from America's #1 Sales Trainer!

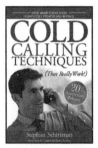
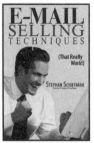

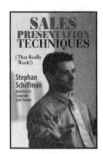

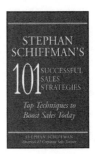

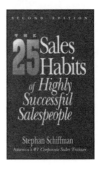

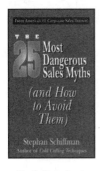
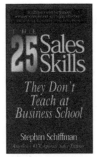

About the Author

Stephan Schiffman is president of D.E.I. Sales Training, one of the largest sales training companies in the United States. He is the author of a number of bestselling books, including *Cold Calling Techniques (That Really Work!)*; *The 25 Most Common Sales Mistakes*; *The 25 Habits of Highly Successful Salespeople*; *Beat Sales Burnout*; *Ask Questions, Get Sales*; *Telesales*; *Closing Techniques (That Really Work!)*; and *The #1 Sales Team*. Schiffman's articles have appeared in the *Wall Street Journal*, the *New York Times*, and *INC.* magazine. He has also appeared as a guest on CNBC, CBNN, CNNfn, and Fox News. For more information about Schiffman and D.E.I. Franchise Systems, Inc., call 1-800-224-2140 or visit *www.dei-sales.com*.